The Neuroscience of Gratitude: Why Self-Help Has It All Wrong

Rewire Your Brain With a Science-Backed Gratitude Practice in 5 Minutes a Day and Develop Positivity, Optimism, Resilience, and Happiness

Andrew Humington

© Copyright 2023 - All rights reserved.

The content contained within this book may not be reproduced, duplicated, or transmitted without direct written permission from the author or the publisher.

Under no circumstances will any blame or legal responsibility be held against the publisher, or author, for any damages, reparation, or monetary loss due to the information contained within this book, either directly or indirectly.

Legal Notice:

This book is copyright protected. It is only for personal use. You cannot amend, distribute, sell, use, quote, or paraphrase any part, or the content within this book, without the consent of the author or publisher.

Disclaimer Notice:

Please note the information contained within this document is for educational and entertainment purposes only. All effort has been executed to present accurate, up-to-date, reliable, and complete information. No warranties of any kind are declared or implied. Readers acknowledge that the author is not engaged in the rendering of legal, financial, medical, or professional advice. The content within this book has been derived from various sources. Please consult a licensed professional before attempting any techniques outlined in this book.

By reading this document, the reader agrees that under no circumstances is the author responsible for any losses, direct or indirect, that are incurred as a result of the use of the information contained within this document, including, but not limited to, errors, omissions, or inaccuracies.

Dear Reader,

Thank you for giving "The Neuroscience of Gratitude" a chance.

But before we get started, we have unadvertised gifts for you:

We at the NeuroMastery Lab would like to offer you these welcoming gifts to thank you for your trust and your love for neuroscience and to help you make the most out of your potential.

Visit Neuromasterylab.com to get all of the following bonuses, FOR FREE!

Your Free Gift n°1:

The Neuroscience of Morning Routine: How to Increase Dopamine and Motivation

A Science-backed protocol to wake up early, increase energy & testosterone, and prevent afternoon slump for men and women.

Morning routines are all the rage. With countless YouTube videos featuring 20-something "gurus" rehashing the same cliches, it's hard to know what's reliable.

Are they genuinely knowledgeable? Or merely seeking clicks and views?

In this practical guide, we decided to study and compile the latest findings of neuroscience to identify the most effective, evidence-based practices.

Discover how to start your day in the most optimal way with science-backed habits, routines, and protocols.

Download It For Free At Neuromasterylab.com

Your Free Gift n°2:

The Checklist For Your Perfect Neuroscientific Morning Routine

To support you in your implementation of the strategies in "The Neuroscience of Morning Routines," we've created this easy-to-follow checklist to guide your morning routine.

Download It For Free At Neuromasterylab.com

Your Free Gift n°3:

The Neuroscience Of Dopamine Detox

Why Dopamine Fasting Usually Doesn't Work And What To Do Instead To Reset Your Dopamine Levels, Take Back Control Of Your Brain And End Laziness

You've likely heard of Dopamine Detox.

In a world filled with endless stimulation and cheap dopamine sources (social media, smartphones, porn, sugary foods), our brains are struggling to keep up. It's easy to become addicted, leading to sluggishness, lack of motivation, and decreased productivity.

Dopamine detox gurus suggest fasting, social media breaks, and phone restrictions to reset dopamine levels and reclaim motivation. While our primitive brains do struggle with modern addictions, is this really an effective solution?

In this concise guide, we explore the neuroscience behind dopamine detox, debunk myths, and provide effective strategies for long-term success.

Read it, and you'll soon have an easy-to-implement protocol at your disposal that will help you gain back control over your brain... and your life.

And perhaps more importantly, you'll be able to stick to it long-term instead of constantly relapsing.

Download It For Free At Neuromasterylab.com

Your Free Gift n°4:

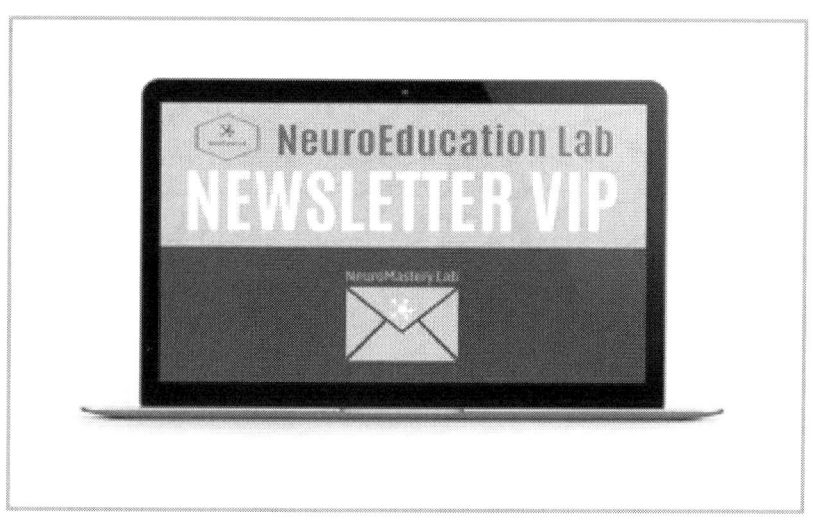

Your free subscription to the Neuroeducation Lab VIP newsletter.

Stay updated with fascinating neuroscience findings and breakthroughs, helping you better understand yourself and your brain. Receive updates on our latest books and publications, along with access to launch pricing and exclusive, time-limited promotions.

<u>Download It For Free At Neuromasterylab.com</u>

Thank you again for your trust; we hope you'll enjoy all these "surprise" bonuses!

Table of Contents

INTRODUCTION 9

CHAPTER 1: THE BENEFITS OF PRACTICING GRATITUDE BACKED BY NEUROSCIENCE 15

A. The Grateful Brain: How Gratitude Benefits Your Life 16

CHAPTER 2: AN IN-DEPTH LOOK INTO NEUROSCIENCE AND GRATITUDE 30

A. Gratitude and the Brain 31
B. Gratitude and the Nervous System 39

CHAPTER 3: THE LIMITATIONS AND NEGATIVE EFFECTS OF TRADITIONAL GRATITUDE PRACTICES 43

A. The Self-Help Gratitude Spiral: Invalidating Our Experiences and Emotions 45

CHAPTER 4: THE MOST EFFECTIVE GRATITUDE PRACTICE BACKED BY NEUROSCIENCE 53

A. Wired For Dark and Light: How Our Neural Circuitry Can Be Rewired 55
B. Highlighting the Differences Between Traditional and True Gratitude 59
C. Creating Your Own Brain Changing Gratitude Practice 65
D. Your Gratitude Protocol Checklist 70

CHAPTER 5: OVERCOMING BARRIERS TO GRATITUDE PRACTICE 76

A. The Ungrateful Brain 79
B. Enhancing Self-Awareness Through Mindfulness Practices 81
C. Neuroscience-Backed Mindfulness 88

CHAPTER 6: MAKING GRATITUDE A LONG-TERM HABIT 92

A. Dealing With the Tough Times and Our Negative Emotions 97
B. Developing Gratitude: Self-Discipline When Motivation Wanes .. 102

CONCLUSION 107
GLOSSARY 112
REFERENCES 116

Introduction

Life can feel like a complex, swirling, and maddening journey, but, if we allow ourselves to be curious, it can have moments of awe and fascination too. Our existence can sometimes feel like a roller coaster of whirlwind experiences, emotions, obstacles, and challenges we need to overcome.

Life is an enigma that is both captivating and exhausting—an intricate dance in which we're processing our environment, juggling our responsibilities, and existing in a world that requires our perpetual and constant engagement.

Our deadlines and expectations loom over us like spectral shadows, while the constant buzz of the smartphone tugs at us—the leash that binds us to the unending lists of tasks that seem to multiply endlessly.

It can all feel like we're a hamster on a wheel, endlessly running to a destination that we will know we'll never truly get to.

And, in the background, the omnipresent hum of the media and their daily dose of doom and gloom subtly assaults our senses and our psyche, reminding us of humanity's crises, conflicts, and calamities.

Every time we open our phones, social media and the internet feed us this information via our screens—hot headlines, breaking news, and potential catastrophes that all add to our stress and anxiety.

As much as we try to filter this depressing information from our lives, it's not long before we're fully submerged, sinking deeper and deeper into an ocean of stress and anxiety. The world outside feels chaotic, unfriendly, and overwhelming, and the simple joy of thriving is long forgotten... replaced with mere existence.

The issue with simply existing is that we inevitably begin to feel stuck. Eventually, the effort to remove ourselves from the Grand Canyon of ruts we're in is so insurmountable that we tell ourselves it'll be easier to remain comfortable in our misery than it to climb out of the painful situations we're experiencing.

If this all sounds too familiar to you; if you're in the midst of this turmoil, life can begin to swallow you whole.

And, if you've spoken to a friend about how you feel, or perhaps your therapist or a self-help book has offered guidance, the primary piece of advice you may have been given is, "Practice gratitude."

This, of course, is not new advice.

In fact, it's as old as time, echoed through religious texts, spiritual teachings, and well-intentioned self-help books. Practicing gratitude seems simple—inviting even.

You're told to count your blessings, focus on the good in your life, and don your rose-tinted glasses so that your perspective on your family, your health, the opportunities you've been given, and your whole outlook on life change.

This is great! It begins to work for you as you reflect on the blessings in your life: Your family and the people who have stood by you through thick and thin, the love you've given and received, your prosperity, in whatever form you've been fortunate enough to receive it, and your health which is highlighted as the most invaluable asset you've granted. You focus on these positives each day. You even write them down in a journal, trying to anchor them deep into your brain, waiting for the day the *gratitude magic* begins, and you no longer need to sift through the endless irritations and obstacles of your life.

But it never comes, does it?

You begin to question your techniques, wondering whether or not you've done something wrong in your practice and that's why your life has not been transformed in the way it was promised it would.

The weight of life—its pressures and challenges—continues to grow, and the shadow of the perpetual stress looms over you, larger than it ever was. And now you feel like a failure because the magic of gratitude didn't work for you. You're left staring at your reflection, wondering, "Is that all there is?"

"Am I doing something wrong?"

If any of this is resonating with you... if you're reading this introduction and in the recesses of your mind, a voice tells you, "We've done all of this, and it doesn't work!" I want you to know you're not alone and the reason gratitude didn't work for you is not your fault. The fact that you have this book and that you're not prepared to give up just yet is admirable, and I'm here to let you know there is a better way to practice gratitude.

I wrote *The Neuroscience of Gratitude: Why Self-Help Has It All Wrong* because I want you to know that once you decode the practice of gratitude, you'll find it's not just another self-help suggestion—it's a potent tool in your arsenal for happiness and fulfillment.

I won't ask you to trust me or take my word.

Instead, I will take this journey with you, diving into the depths of your brain so that we can debunk some widely accepted myths and misconceptions about gratitude. You will be guided through the process of using gratitude as a tool in a way that is backed by neuroscience, and using studies that show you exactly how to change the way your brain thinks.

You see, gratitude is very much like developing your own superpower. A power you never knew existed but is lying dormant in your mind, and when wielded correctly, your gratitude superpower can reshape your world in truly astonishing ways.

I'd like you to take a moment and visualize your life if you could wake up every day with unshakeable positivity and a buoyant optimism tinting your world with the colors of hope and possibility. If you could face the trials and tribulations of life, not with dread, but with resilience and tenacity, turning adversity into opportunity.

Now, imagine developing a sense of fulfillment that fills up your life, making each moment of each day resonate with a deep, profound sense of purpose. This is the power of *gratitude* and it's all within your grasp if you know *why* and *how* gratitude works!

Here's the thing, the benefits of gratitude are not just psychological. They span across all areas of your life—from the physical to the professional and even the spiritual—that are touched by the stress and anxiety of modern life. On a physiological level, gratitude can bolster your immune system, enhance your sleep quality, and reduce your pain sensitivity. Professionally, a consistent practice of gratitude will leave you brimming with motivation, while your productivity soars and decision-making processes occur with ease and clarity. Spiritually, gratitude deepens your sense of purpose and meaning and can finally help you uncover that piece of your life that has eluded you for so long. It empowers your personal compass that continually guides you toward personal growth and appreciation for your life and life in its entirety.

And, gratitude helps you draw people closer, strengthen your bonds, and foster great communication with those you value in your life. With proper gratitude practices, you can improve your empathy, trust, and mutual respect. Whether it's your romantic partner, family, friends, or professional acquaintances, you'll begin to exude such a strong positive energy that people around you will gravitate toward you, responding positively to your new-found attitude to life.

Now I'm not denying that all of this can sound too good to be true. It may feel like you've heard all of these claims before. If you're a skeptic, you may believe there is a catch somewhere, and the truth is that there is... but the catch is you and your willingness to open your mind to the scientifically proven benefits of gratitude.

So what is the difference between this book and all of the "how-tos" listed online or the self-help guru's expert advice that drives the billion-dollar self-help industry? Most of the information available in the self-help market merely grazes the surface of what gratitude truly is and brushes over how to practice it. I'd like to make it clear that everything you've heard before wasn't entirely wrong but using this information is like putting on a pair of skis and expecting to become an expert skier. You're only receiving part of the message, some of the instructions, and the promise of results from an incomplete manual to one of the greatest neurological tools available to you.

The human brain needs to know details of *how* to practice something, as well as *why* you're doing it. Your brain needs a *purpose* which is the conundrum that needs to be unraveled when it comes to proper gratitude practice. Science provides a deeper understanding of this purpose as well as how it works while creating new neural pathways. And this is the journey you're going to take with me—deep into the latest findings of neuroscience to see what gratitude is and what it is not.

This journey will be one that is enlightening and exhilarating as we pull back the curtain on gratitude, revealing the truth that's been hidden in plain sight, challenging long-held beliefs, and smashing old paradigms. More importantly, you will learn a remarkably potent form of practicing gratitude that has been largely overlooked so that you can implement it through a simple *Gratitude Protocol* in 5 steps.

Even better, it takes only 5 minutes of practice a day to see profound changes happening to your life and your world. So if you're ready to unveil the potent power of gratitude that lies dormant within you—to step into a new world brimming with positivity, purpose, and fulfillment—then dive into *The Neuroscience of Gratitude* with me right now.

Chapter 1: The Benefits of Practicing Gratitude Backed By Neuroscience

Ask anyone what they really want for their lives, and they'll probably reply with, "I want to be happy, content, or experience inner peace," at least once. And that's great, really it is, but this happiness, contentment, and inner peace is subjective, isn't it? Your pursuit of happiness is not a cookie-cutter definition that fits all people, nor should it be.

That perfect career, the white picket fence, two-point-five children, or friends that contribute meaningfully to your life all sound so idyllic. It's the American dream that has been commercialized and sold the world over as the standard for what happiness is. We fill our lives with material things and standards of happiness, measuring our joy by our wealth, a new car, or the partner on our arm, and we disregard the fact that our definition of happiness is not anyone else's.

We walk through life wondering what it means to be happy, practicing gratitude for all of these things we've accumulated that should define whether or not we're thriving in our lives. Worse, we force ourselves to feel gratitude for them so that we can dig ourselves out of the rut we find ourselves in and say thank you for a life we have built on someone else's values, purpose, and definition of success.

At its roots, gratitude is meant to be the art of being thankful, but there are millions of people the world over who are saying thank you for a (metaphorical) dry, stale loaf of bread when what they really wanted was a double cheeseburger and fries.

Now, let me make it clear that I am not saying gratitude doesn't work. It does! In fact, gratitude is so powerful it changes the very structure of the human brain.

Throughout this chapter, I'll show you how beneficial gratitude really is to your life. But first, you need to acknowledge that gratitude based on someone else's definition of life, or love, or success, or anything else for that matter, will never resonate with you.

You need to learn to turn inward, become self-reflective, and truly decide what it is that you want for your life and how you define joy or inner peace. This definition of an ideal life is one piece of the puzzle you need to begin practicing gratitude in the way it should be practiced.

Another piece is knowing *how* gratitude works on a physiological and neurological level.

It's all well and good knowing that gratitude can make you feel amazing, boost your productivity and mood, and even cure physiological ailments, but without the how it's all just going to sound like some esoteric fairytale that belongs on a shelf in the recess of your mind. However, thanks to studies conducted on the effects of gratitude (not just on the human psyche but our physiology too), we now know just how incredible true gratitude can be for our health and well-being.

A. The Grateful Brain: How Gratitude Benefits Your Life

We will explore the human brain and gratitude in further depth in Chapter 4, unraveling the chemical and physiological changes that occur when practicing gratitude correctly. For now, you're just going to need to know the basics of how your brain works and what centers of the brain are affected when gratitude is practiced. This information will provide you with a deeper understanding of not only the benefits of gratitude but also *why* changes occur that are beneficial to your physical and mental health.

The first thing you need to know is that the human brain is a marvelously complex organ that is responsible for everything from temperature control to motor function. Our thoughts, memories, emotions, senses, and the basic functions that keep us alive are all handled by the brain. They consist of white matter and gray matter that each house a different region and serves a different function. Gray matter is the outer portion of the brain, while white matter is the inner portion. The gray matter is made up of neuron somas and axons which connect neurons together, as well as myelin. Every region in the brain serves a different purpose, and our gray matter as a whole is responsible for interpreting information and processing this information. The brain requires a complex balance of chemicals and electrical signals to work properly and ensure we remain mentally and physically well. But why is this important to know when speaking about gratitude?

Well, science shows that gratitude, when practiced consistently and properly, changes brain function, improving cognitive functions. The reason that these changes occur is that gratitude primarily engages the prefrontal cortex.

Our prefrontal cortex is the most evolved brain region, which means it serves as the area that dictates our highest-order cognitive abilities, including problem-solving, memory, analytical thinking, critical thinking, evaluation, and metacognition. Our prefrontal cortex is directly responsible for assessing our environment and creating our perceptions and beliefs about life. It also means that what we feel, whether negative or positive, has the ability to affect our brains and that since our brain never loses the ability to learn, adapt, or develop, changing these thoughts and perceptions changes the structure of our brains and how they work.

If it were as easy as putting on a pair of rose-tinted glasses, everyone would practice gratitude, though, and if you're reading this book, there's a pretty significant chance you've already given gratitude a go, only to find it didn't work.

Why?

It's because our perception of life is based on a deeply rooted belief system that has formed over time through habits as well as external reinforcement. Belief systems are the single most powerful (and often detrimental) part of our psyche, and without first changing our beliefs, our brains will continue to push an agenda that simply isn't factual.

Think about it: A thousand years ago, human beings believed fire was given to humans by a god, and it was only through curiosity and being able to shed this belief that the true source of fire was uncovered. Simply writing things down, saying affirmations, and digging deep to find the things that went right in our lives doesn't change our beliefs, nor does it encourage us to be curious about our lives. Practicing gratitude without changing our beliefs is like denying our house is on fire because the flames haven't reached where we're sitting yet.

Uncovering your belief systems and seeking to change them will be discussed in later chapters, but for now, you have the basic information needed on how your brain works and why gratitude may not have worked for you before.

It's no secret that human beings somaticize their feelings. If we're stressed, our muscles become tense, we ache, headaches develop, and over time, more dire issues like high blood pressure begin to become chronic ailments. The same can be said for the reverse—when we feel great, our bodies tend to play along, we feel more alert and healthy, and even our physical appearance seems to change (in our eyes at least).

Physiological data seems to support the notion that psychological conditioning has long and short-term implications for our bodies, even including our organs. Modern medical technology that examines inflammation markers as well as brain mapping using magnetic resonance imaging (MRI) indicates that significant positive changes occur within the brain when practicing gratitude correctly.

As a result of these physiological changes, emotional regulation and stress tolerance increase, causing a direct positive effect on overall well-being, improved sleep quality, and a reduction in the symptoms of depression and anxiety.

While all of this may sound like pseudoscience, psychosomatic illness is a well-known phenomenon that most people have some understanding of. So why do we believe that this psychosomatic response could not occur when positive feelings are the driving force behind physical and mental well-being?

1. *Psychological Benefits of Gratitude*

We live in a society where our mood is governed by external forces that cause us to idealize a life that isn't truly ours. We prioritize the needs of others and believe that our joy is dependent on the lives others have built for themselves. And, when our mood doesn't lift because we live in a cloud of expectation for what *could* be, we head off to a physician to be prescribed a pill that will make it all go away, in the hopes that pharmaceuticals may change the chemical makeup of our brains.

Neuroscience tells us that our brains are designed to problem-solve and to critically think our way out of challenges and obstacles in order for us to be truly appreciative of what we have accumulated and accomplished. In other words, our brains are wired to find reward in struggle, and for gratitude to work, this system of thought needs to be overridden.

Gratitude, when practiced properly, changes the neural structures of the brain, making us feel more content and joyful (Ackerman, 2018). Of course, our ancestors understood the value of gratitude but devoid of modern technology and pressures, it seemed these philosophies surrounding "the mother of all human feelings" were less complicated than modern people make them out to be.

Pioneers in neuropsychological research, however, have begun studying gratitude once more as a marker for mental health, and with modern medical technology now aiding them, some astounding psychological benefits have been uncovered. Because gratitude triggers the release of feel-good hormones in the brain, it also effectively activates its reward center, altering our perception of the world. A simple thank you is enough to direct the brain to pay attention to the behavior that triggered this hormone release and drives us to repeat this behavior.

In other words, gratitude is the catalyst for the release of powerful neurochemical transmitters like dopamine, norepinephrine, and serotonin, all of which are the brain and body's management systems for our emotions, appropriate stress responses, and anxiety. Added to this, gratitude creates a complex chain of neural mechanisms in the brain, developing new neural pathways, synaptic connections, and strengthening the behaviors that promote a reward.

Continuous (proper) gratitude affects a number of areas in the brain, but interestingly, the right temporal cortex, which manages and regulates emotions, begins to change, creating a phenomenon known as synaptic plasticity within the brain. This development of the temporal cortex creates higher volumes of gray matter and a balanced release of neurochemicals.

Essentially, our brain has the ability to produce a natural antidepressant that is on par with most chemical pharmaceuticals on the market (Kong et al., 2019). In fact, when practiced often, gratitude has a longer-lasting effect than pharmaceuticals because the practice affects our brain's on a neurotransmitter level.

As such, gratitude reduces not only the stress hormones present in our bodies but also helps manage the autonomic nervous system's functions, reducing the symptoms of both anxiety and depression through the release of neurochemicals.

These same neurochemicals are responsible for the modulation of our prefrontal cortex, which processes emotions we view as negative, including shame, guilt, blame, and so on. When the amygdala and hippocampus receive these neurochemicals, better emotional regulation occurs, and an overall feeling of sustained well-being begins to form.

With the release of feel-good hormones comes the lowering of cortisol to within biologically acceptable levels, and stress tolerance increases, allowing us to better handle the stressful situations modern life throws our way. This enables us to reframe negative experiences on a neurological level without conscious effort or having to place effort into appreciating the little things that have gone right.

2. *Physical Benefits of Gratitude*

The physical benefits of proper gratitude practice are not pseudoscience, as some believe. Gratitude may not have a direct effect on our health, but a healthy mind drives a healthy body and vice versa.

It's a conundrum... A chicken and egg situation in which science isn't even sure whether the brain decides how healthy the body is or if the body simply tells the brain. What science is abundantly clear on is that lowered stress, depression, and anxiety have a positive effect on our physiological being, and this is perhaps where gratitude promotes health benefits.

While gratitude cannot possibly have a direct physical effect on the body, it does have a positive influence on the brain, which of course, has physiological effects. Because anxiety, stress, and fear are the driving forces for most of modern people's chronic aches, pains, and illnesses, it would make sense that taking psychological action against the lifestyle conditions like stress would increase the body's well-being.

Proper management of stress directly reduces both anxiety and fear and increases a person's resistance to everyday stressors and challenges. It is in this stress management that we can see the benefits of gratitude on the body. With the vast amount of research conducted into stress and the physical reactions surrounding the body's stress responses, it shouldn't come as a surprise that being under chronic stress worsens a host of medical conditions.

These conditions, including anxiety, depression, cardiac disease, neurodegenerative disease, certain cancers, and so on, may come about suddenly or develop over time, and have the ability to become chronic if not properly addressed.

The exact mechanisms of how stress induces diseases in the human body may remain somewhat of a medical and scientific mystery, but the facts irrevocably conclude that stress is a leading factor to entirely too many preventable illnesses.

Research conducted in 2017 showed that inflammation, a chronic response to stress, may be at the root of these illnesses as a result of the hormones and chemicals released into the body. This same research showed that chronic stress is often avoidable when using stress management techniques like yoga, deep breathing, and, you guessed it—gratitude (Liu et al., 2017). To better understand the physical benefits of gratitude on the body, we must, therefore, examine the mechanisms of stress that affect people and how the brain reacts to stress.

The Body and Stress

Emotional and physical stress triggers the brain's evolutionary fight or flight response, a physiological process that is designed to keep us safe by either fighting off danger or fleeing from it. This physiological effect begins with the perception and interpretation of a threat, encouraging the brain to release the stress hormone cortisol. When this hormone is released, it suppresses non-essential functions, like the immune system, diverting the body's resources to the production of glucose and adrenaline, as well as heightening our senses and encouraging a faster heartbeat and shallow breathing.

Now, it's important to note that properly managed stress is great. It encourages short bursts of productivity and efficiency. When subjected to constant stress, however, the body remains in a "diverted" state, stealing resources from vital body systems like the immune system.

You may already be aware that your immune system is required to fight off bacteria, viruses, and other microbiota that enter into it, but it is also responsible for the healing of the tissues and organs in the body, especially when an injury or disease has occurred.

This healing process occurs after the body triggers an inflammatory response to the disease or injury, signaling the immune system to send out pro-inflammatory cytokines that attack invaders of the body and tissue that is damaged beyond repair so that the body can produce new, healthy tissue.

Inflammation isn't pleasant and often comes with pain, but it is required for the body to heal itself effectively. Temporary inflammation, like stress, is a necessary bodily function to keep us healthy and safe, but chronic inflammation and a suppressed immune system present a much larger issue. When inflammation is chronic and pervades our bodies, they behave as if we're sick, causing all of our systems to respond as if we have a virus. In the absence of any virus to attack though, the immune system upregulates itself, attacking healthy cells, creating pain, and the formation of a stress loop begins.

The cycle of stress is a self-propagating one: Stress creates inflammation, and inflammation causes stress. Without intervention in the form of proper stress management, like gratitude, this cycle will continue unimpeded.

With that in mind, gratitude was studied to help understand how psychological practices can be used to reduce chronic conditions in the body, like inflammation and pain, as well as the subsequent damage to the bones, joints, and organs as a result of stress. Gratitude as a trend in the self-help industry hasn't done much for the practice as far as the everyday person on the street is concerned, but science and medicine are fervently studying and uncovering the reasons gratitude makes the body more healthy. Growing bodies of research show that gratitude, when practiced correctly, improves sleep, lowers stress, and as a side effect, improves overall health, including a reduction in inflammation and chronic diseases (Chaplin et al., 2018).

In fact, gratitude seems to decrease everything from disease to materialism, which is interesting from a psychological perspective because people who are stressed and living in a *lack* mindset often accumulate things rather than understanding that they already have everything they need to be happy and joyful. Another study showed that gratitude helped lower the risk of heart disease, because of a reduction in chronic cortisol levels, and improved the symptoms of depression caused by chronic cardiovascular disease (Fritz et al., 2019).

Research has also suggested that those who practice gratitude have a 16% reduction in pain once the practice was properly instituted, and this percentage increased as respondents regularly incorporated gratitude into their lives. In fact, many of the respondents in this study went on to make remarkable recoveries as their mindset to pain changed and other physical exercises were incorporated into their lifestyle, further reducing pain (Harvard Health Publishing, 2021).

Inflammation in people who practiced gratitude was substantially lower than in those who did not. This lowered inflammatory response seemed to directly correspond with the onset of proper gratitude, and participants in one particular study showed remarkable recovery times from common diseases like the flu, as well as a vast reduction in inflammation markers for people who had otherwise suffered from long-term diseases including diabetes, Lupus, and other autoimmune disorders (University of Utah, 2021).

While the physiological benefits of gratitude for the body indisputably begin in the brain, we cannot turn a blind eye to the fact that gratitude, as a whole, improves well-being.

3. The Social and Relational Benefits of Gratitude

Social belonging is a basic human need as identified by Maslow's hierarchy of needs (Bartlett & DeSteno, 2006). Enhancing our social bonds and strengthening our relationships increases positive emotions within us, improves our relationship satisfaction, and makes it more likely that we feel valued enough in our relationships to reciprocate empathy, love, and trust.

Now, I am by no means claiming that gratitude is a cure-all when it comes to the development of healthy relationships, but it is an inspiring and highly valuable tool that can be used in the meaningful creation, maintenance, and development of social relationships.

The relationship between social connection and gratitude is not a new one, and neurological research has explored the intricate relationship between the multifaceted aspects of social connection and gratitude. These studies show that there is strong evidence that gratitude works on the perception level that interlinks the visual and sensory areas of our brains with the frontal lobe. This means mental representations of our environment, including stimuli, begin to integrate with the prefrontal cortex and include our amygdala and hippocampus, which are responsible for our thoughts and beliefs.

I want to make it clear that this process occurs every day without gratitude practice, and whether or not we're aware of it, our brain is creating a perception of our reality every second of every day. Perception and reality differ, but in the human brain, our perception forms our reality. Have you ever noticed that what you focus on or perceive to be annoying or disrespectful tends to amplify?

Shoes are not placed in their proper place one time, and suddenly all you see are your partner's shoes lying everywhere. You notice a little clutter in one room and suddenly your home begins to feel overwhelmingly filthy...

Our brain is a master at creating a reality we program it to see through our insistence on noticing certain stimuli, behaviors, and subconscious thoughts. And, when we begin to insist on negative perceptions, we begin to catastrophize things, developing an all-or-nothing way of life. We start to think, "They *will* put away their shoes because if they don't, they're *disrespecting* me and my needs!" This kind of thinking is incredibly damaging, not only for the psyche of the person holding onto the beliefs but for the people in interpersonal relationships with them.

What gratitude does is change our perception of the world, altering our reality and training our minds to see the value in the people we surround ourselves with. All of this strengthens our social bonds, reinforcing our connections with others and increasing our desire to remain neutral when evaluating strangers within our environment (Algoe et al., 2010).

Don't believe me?

Take a moment to reflect upon your life and how many opportunities you may have missed because of cynicism, fear, or bias. Now, ask yourself how many of these opportunities you would have welcomed if you were simply grateful to be presented with them—no judgment, no cynicism, just pure gratitude. How much healthier, wealthier, more connected, and even happier do you think you would be right now?

I'm not asking these questions so that you beat yourself up, nor is it too late to change and embrace gratitude for the powerful tool it is. And if you still don't believe me, write this moment down so that you can revisit it in a few weeks, months, or years after practicing proper gratitude and see how your life has changed.

Added to this, gratitude is beneficial to our sense of social responsibility, encouraging us to display more prosocial behaviors within a diverse community of people. Diversity, of course, exposes us to different viewpoints and perspectives, which in turn, encourages us to become more empathetic to the plight of others (Bartlett & DeSteno, 2006).

Empathy and the understanding that others want to interact with us on a more meaningful level provides us with a reason behind the creation of interpersonal relationships. We become more likely to feel that we deserve to be treated with dignity, respect, and kindness in the same way we treat others. Often, the very fact that we have developed amazing relationships based on gratitude reinforces this notion, as others are more prepared to offer support and be helpful because of the way they are treated (Wood et al., 2010).

And all of this, of course, leads us to why gratitude is beneficial to you and your well-being.

For us to truly experience a sense of well-being, we need to embrace all the facets of what it means to be well. We cannot hit the gym three times a week and eat healthy if our mind is unwell, nor can we expect to feel a sense of well-being if our relationships are falling apart.

Well-being is holistic and includes our mental, physical, social, intellectual, emotional, occupational, spiritual, cultural, financial, and environmental health. While some of these aspects, like our intellectual, environmental, and emotional well-being, are logically within our control, we tend to forget that every facet of our well-being is technically an attainable goal.

Gratitude, when practiced properly, is so powerful that people are more likely to experience financial and occupational well-being (Marquit et al., 2023). Gratitude has even been associated with improved intellectual well-being too (Sansone & Sansone, 2019).

This brings us back to whether or not gratitude is the key to unlocking inner joy and peace. I cannot provide a definitive answer to that question, but I can say that science provides irrefutable proof of how gratitude can positively influence a person's life. Through small actions and proper knowledge, gratitude can change the very structure of the human brain.

When practiced regularly, gratitude leads to functional changes in a number of areas of the brain, leading to improved processing of our emotions, inner dialogue, and how we interact with others. The brain's neural pathways, over time, strengthen throughout the practice of gratitude, rewiring our minds to *see*, not seek out, the positive in life.

And this, of course, all means that we become happier, healthier, more loveable people without having to put conscious effort into persistently looking for joy or wading through the metaphorical manure we believe our lives to be so that we can find a tiny nugget of gold.

Instead, we become active participants in our own lives rather than being a victim of it—we remove the blindfold of programmed despair, and we truly begin to live a joyful, prosperous life.

Chapter 2:
An In-Depth Look Into Neuroscience and Gratitude

Throughout Chapter 1, we discussed the benefits of gratitude and how some of the ways in which the practice can alter the very structure and chemical makeup of our brains. Briefly brushing over this remarkable neurological change is not sufficient though, and for us to truly understand the power of gratitude, it's imperative that we take a deeper dive into exactly what gratitude does to the brain and nervous system.

In this chapter, we'll be diving deep in order to uncover exactly what it is that gratitude does to our brains on a neurological level and the role it plays in our nervous system.

Through scientific research conducted in the field of neuroscience, we can begin to understand the role of the brain's reward pathway and how the release of powerful neurotransmitters like dopamine and serotonin improves our feelings of well-being and other positive emotions.

When we develop a deeper understanding of how the different areas of our brain are activated when practicing gratitude and the subsequent changes that occur, gratitude begins to make more sense, and we are provided with both the *why* and the *how* of the practice.

Once we know all of this information, we can begin to formulate a clear, concise roadmap to a gratitude practice that is meaningful and beneficial for our lives and the lives of our loved ones. While I did my best to simplify the information below, we're going to get quite technical with what happens in our brains when gratitude is practiced. This information is important, but there is no need to memorize it or fully comprehend what is being said for us to use the gratitude protocol provided later in this book.

With everything I've said in mind—pun intended—let's begin to uncover what gratitude does to the human brain and the enormous potential that lies dormant in the unused recesses of our minds. For those fascinated with science, the findings of studies on proper gratitude and how the brain functions when practicing it are truly fascinating. Having said that, for those who don't enjoy science, or don't want to feel too drowned in facts, feel free to skip the sections below and move on to Chapter 3.

A. Gratitude and the Brain

Collective studies using functional magnetic resonance imaging (fMRI) and MRI imagining over the last few years have begun to merely touch the tip of the iceberg that is the benefits of gratitude.

Neuroscience has, with this new knowledge of the neural system, in fact, shown such remarkable results that the industry has developed an entirely new vocabulary of words, including neuroleadership, neuromarketing, and even neuroinfluence. Before I get into what these studies show for people like you and me, I want to show you what neuroscience circles found when they branched into leadership and organizational frameworks to test the effects of gratitude among leadership influencers and employees.

The results were astounding!

Respondents within an established leadership group who were taught to practice proper gratitude showed an increase in neuron density and, subsequently, a much higher level of emotional intelligence than established leaders not practicing gratitude. Among employees, gratitude also increased neuron density, and with the corporate rewards and recognition programs suggested by neuroscientists, organizations increased the number of employees expressing gratitude, even outside of the respondent test group. All of this, of course, meant that they began to benefit from higher levels of neural knowledge and an overall increase in psychological capital within the organization (Kini et al., 2016).

What neuroscience has done for gratitude is the ability to know what the brain looks like when practicing gratitude. And when we know how the brain responds to gratitude in real-time, and we mix in the neurochemicals that make us feel happy, the true power of gratitude begins to unfold.

These neurochemicals are a good place to start when trying to understand the human brain, its reward center, and the neurochemicals that elevate our mood.

When expressing gratitude for what's great in our lives or by showing gratitude to others, the neural circuitry within our brain, and more specifically the brain stem, is stimulated to produce dopamine, a feel-good neurochemical that is produced in three areas of the brain.

One of these three areas is the substantia nigra, an area of the brain that is absolutely critical in the production of dopamine. Now dopamine isn't only responsible for elevating our mood and giving us a good ol 'shot of happy hormones. It also has a direct, positive effect on the central nervous system, which controls everything from cognitive executive functions to movement, and emotional regulation.

But more on that later in this chapter.

Here's the thing about dopamine, it makes us feel happy... Euphoric even, and this means we want more. The reward center of the brain is activated, and we feel more optimistic about, well, just about everything. This is critical to know because when the reward center is activated, the brain changes our behaviors so that we can experience this euphoria again, and over time, these new behaviors lead to natural motivation as well as improved productivity and performance. Dopamine isn't the only neurochemical involved in this process though, and gratitude also encourages the release of serotonin from the anterior cingulate cortex. This powerful chemical is a messenger that is directly responsible for a whole host of different functions like sleep, digestion, mood, bone health, satisfaction, motivation, and willpower. Serotonin is our body's natural mood enhancer and has been dubbed the "happy molecule" in science circles.

Neuroscience has already established that neuroplasticity, or the ability to learn new things, continues throughout our lives and that this plasticity is more likely, or perhaps exclusively possible, when the reward center of the brain is activated.

Let's break for a second here so we tie this all together.

Hebbian's theory is a psychological theory that claims, and has been proven true, that when a neural cell is "persistently and repeatedly" stimulated an increase in synaptic efficacy occurs (Josep Calbet, 2018). It's a mouthful, I know, but in simple terms, synapses that are wired together will fire together.

That's good news for practitioners of gratitude because not only are they thriving off the effects of dopamine and serotonin with minimal effort because the brain is taking care of motivation and willpower, but their gray matter is increasing, the brain is becoming more receptive to knowledge and skills, and the emotional and rational centers of the brain are no longer at war. The quelling of this war is also an important side note because once the rational mind is balanced with the emotional one, and vice versa, we begin to operate from the wise mind.

Why is this important?

According to Maslow's hierarchy of needs which is the pyramid of human needs that should be fulfilled in order for us to be truly happy and content in life, self-actualization is the final and most critical of our needs when it comes to true fulfillment. While our other needs, like sustenance, shelter, social belonging, and such, are almost always automatically taken care of by ourselves or others, self-actualization is often never attained as we chase the eternal pot of gold at the end of a rainbow that doesn't belong to us. This means there are a whole lot of unfulfilled adults roaming the globe pondering all of the reasons they just don't feel content, even if they have everything their human heart desires.

Back to the question—why is it important that we operate from the wise mind? This is where self-actualization occurs, and gratitude is the key that unlocks the very recesses of our wise minds.

Now, it's important to remember that neural pathways that are wired together don't only work for the positive things in life. In fact, being negative and only noticing how hard the world is, reinforces neural pathways too. It's a bad habit and one that's extremely hard to break because these neural pathways are pretty well established. Thinking negatively and immersing ourselves in all things negative becomes our default mode, creating more negativity and ultimately reinforcing the very neural pathways that are the source of our negative thinking.

Don't panic, all is not lost! We need to be able to shift how we think so that we can incorporate as much of the brain as we can while stimulating the production of dopamine and serotonin for new neural pathways to lay down a brand new super highway in our brains, replacing the old, beaten down, negative pathways in our minds. Our brains lap up these neurochemicals, and because of this, we need dopamine and serotonin to reinforce positivity. Sure, it's tough in the beginning, but the more we give ourselves this neurochemical boost, the more positivity and optimism become our default response, and the weaker our negative pathways become.

And it's precisely this serotonin and dopamine boost that is the foundation of the gratitude practices you will learn in this book so that you can begin to form positive neural pathways without invalidating the negative or having to desperately search for something positive that happened in your day.

1. Gratitude: Laying a New Neural Highway

Our emotions and our motivations are closely related constructs within the brain and influence our cognitive performance, our reactions, and our behaviors. In layman's terms, our emotions have both a psychological and physiological effect on our bodies, and how we feel will inevitably influence how we behave (Lang, 2010).

It's cause and effect. Breaking Lang's concept down further, emotions, therefore, consist of thoughts and feelings (phenomenology), our neurons, neurochemicals, and the physical responses of our bodies and brains (physiology), and our actions, reactions, or readiness to act (our behaviors). And this makes sense, we know that when we feel something, our body reacts, and we express our emotion outwardly, whether with thought or without it. There is, however, a vital fourth state in this emotion-motivation cause and effect that a lot of people experience because of their mindset. Emotivations, as they're called, are a state in which we consciously, and later sub-consciously, set goals to experience an emotion in a specific way (Lang, 2010).

But how is this possible? Emotions are a primal state, aren't they?

Well, yes, but that doesn't mean the brain cannot be trained or programmed to recognize an emotion and act in a specific way. You see, emotions consist not only of processes, but subprocesses too. How we feel in our environment or react to the stimuli we're exposed to is pretty subjective in nature.

One person can stand on the lake shore on a cold, windy day and be programmed to grumble, be upset, and leave in a huff because the weather didn't play along, while another can stand in the wind with a smile on their face and gratitude in their mind.

It's about the construct of our phenomenology first, and if you didn't know it quite yet, thoughts and feelings, not emotions, are manageable and controllable. Your emotions are primal and instinctive and are designed to keep us safe. They're a remanent of your ancestor's days when the dangers in the external world were real and life-threatening. Feelings are what we experience as a result of our emotions. If we experience the emotion anger, and choose to fixate on this anger rather than letting it pass or respond to it accordingly, we can begin to feel irritated, annoyed, or even sad. Feelings, unlike emotions, last as long as we want them to. Thoughts on the other hand are a collection of our past experiences and motivations for certain behaviors and actions. Our thoughts can fuel our feelings and our emotions but our emotions and feelings are not our thoughts. We can think our way into an emotion and we can think our way out of it in the same we we can think our way into our out of feelings.

Gratitude doesn't work on controlling the uncontrollable, not in our brains nor in our environments or our responses. It works with the right areas of the brain to create the right chemicals that activate the reward center of the brain, which in turn builds motivation to be grateful.

In order for anything to work, we need to know where in the brain it works first and how this relates to our intrinsic motivation and behaviors, and thanks to fMRI scans, that's exactly what we've been able to discover about gratitude.

The area of the brain that is linked to decision-making and learning is the medial prefrontal cortex. This area of the brain was keenly studied in relation to gratitude, with two groups being separated and asked two different questions relating to life (Kini et al., 2016). These questions were designed to entice this area of the brain so that neuroscientists could register activity in the medial prefrontal cortex and how sustained the activity in this region was.

The first group was asked to think about a time they were grateful and replay this gratitude in their mind. The second group was asked to recall their gratitude but speak it out loud. These expressions of gratitude were recorded and shared with others. Specifically, the person that the subject was expressing gratitude toward.

While the medial prefrontal cortex did moderately engage in group one, the thinkers, this activity was neither sufficient nor sustained enough for new neural pathways to be laid. Conversely, group two, the outward expressors of gratitude, showed a huge surge of medial prefrontal cortex activity that was completely different from other brain activity. This sustained, powerful activity was shown to be the beginning of neural pathway growth and seems to suggest that gratitude needs to be expressed externally, not just thought internally (Kini et al., 2016).

A second study conducted using fMRI technology sought to explore changes in the ventromedial prefrontal cortex, our brain's altruism and reward center (Karns et al., 2017). When this area of the brain is activated, the brain begins to crave the same experience and will begin to facilitate behaviors that encourage reward and pleasure.

Both groups were requested to journal every day for a period of three weeks, but group one was given prompts that were wholly unrelated to the practice of gratitude, while group two was asked to write about their gratitude experiences in detail.

With three weeks over, groups one and two's fMRI results were compared, and group two showed significant and sustained activity in the ventromedial prefrontal cortex, and new subconscious behaviors had begun to form (Karns et al., 2017). Of course, this proves that the brain requires reward in order to reinforce behavior, but we already knew that. What is fascinating is that pure altruism, or helping others without reward, is an automatic response when the ventromedial prefrontal cortex is activated, showing that gratitude benefits both the person expressing gratitude as well as bystanders.

Yet another study of gratitude as an intervention in depression and the regulations of emotions, conducted in 2017, focused on the amygdala (Karns et al., 2017). This region is specifically known for the processing of emotions and is part of the limbic system, which is one of the oldest areas of our brains from an evolutionary standpoint. This is important to remember when reading the results of all of these research and study efforts into gratitude because it suggests that gratitude itself is an evolutionary emotion, much like joy, anger, or any of the other most rudimentary emotions we feel.

It also means that gratitude, theoretically, is a part of our brain's safety responses that include fight, flight, freeze, and so on. What this study showed, using fMRI technology, is that when respondents focused on gratitude, the amygdala showed activity under the limbic system, engaging and processing both memory and emotions. What is particularly interesting about this study is that fMRI scans were not taken in the process of gratitude but rather when the brain was in a resting state. Now, what's important to note is that when activity occurs under the limbic system it affects all areas of our brain and our nervous system. This is because the limbic system is the cross roads where every message and signal that travels to and from our brain converges, directing information to where it needs to go. With this knowledge, it becomes easier to see the conclusive proof that gratitude continues to work on certain areas of the brain when not actively being thought of or practiced.

With this in mind, researchers went further, moving their attention to the activity of the nucleus accumbens, the modulation center for our limbic and motor systems, in respondents who had been diagnosed with depression (Kyeong et al., 2017). With regular, proper gratitude practice, the nucleus accumbens began to respond positively, the brain corrected neurochemical imbalances naturally, and ultimately the severity and duration of depressive episodes improved.

What all of these studies ultimately suggest is that when the brain is engaged in proper gratitude practices, positive impacts begin to take place throughout not only the brain but the body as well. By creating and reinforcing new neural growth through our conscious behaviors, our brain begins to encourage our body to seek out the neurochemicals that make us feel euphoric, and our brain remains in a state of active gratitude awareness.

Even more fascinating is that the brain responds to gratitude in the same way as it does to other emotions, suggesting gratitude is a somewhat repressed aspect of our internal safety system. And, as we know, repressed emotion can cause extreme issues that ultimately result in dysregulation, mood disorders, and repeated behaviors in an attempt to soothe ourselves from an impending doom that we're actually just creating for ourselves.

B. Gratitude and the Nervous System

The nervous system is a huge network of nerves that send key messages to and from the brain in milliseconds and are responsible for keeping us alive, responding to our environment, our senses, and a whole lot of other functions. Both the sympathetic and parasympathetic systems form part of the nervous system as a whole and dominate our autonomic systems. They are two halves of a whole; the one works in conjunction with the other.

Having said that, each system also works in opposition to the other in order to create balance within the body. For example, the sympathetic nervous system (SNS) is responsible for increasing our heart rate and encouraging oxygen-rich blood faster to the brain and lungs. The SNS is responsible for the physiological effects that occur when we have anxiety or enter into a fight or flight response. The parasympathetic nervous system (PSNS) has the opposite effect, calming our body by lowering our heart rate, slowing breathing, and setting the body into a state of relaxation. This is, of course, a very rudimentary explanation of the nervous system, but it's important to know because it helps us understand why things like our resting heart rate can be a pretty good indication of how well our PSNS is functioning. The PSNS communicates with the brain through the vagus nerve. The very nerve that is responsible for a whole lot of crucial body systems, including our ability to regulate our mood, maintain heart rate, and a proper immune response.

The SNS uses adrenaline, and more specifically norepinephrine, to activate the fight or flight response, and it's this hormone, along with others like cortisol, that causes issues in our body when our organs and brain are exposed to them for long periods of time. The PSNS uses acetylcholine, a hormone responsible for triggering a relaxed state to encourage the vagus nerve to let the body know it's safe.

Now, emotions trigger all of the responses of the nervous system that aren't responsible for survival. So we're not talking about breathing, digestion, or a heartbeat here, but it is important that you understand a prolonged state of stress puts unnecessary strain on the organs associated with the fight or flight response.

We have already established that gratitude appears to be an evolutionary emotion that affects the areas of the brain that process memories and emotions, as well as the physical and mental stimuli that trigger emotions. Added to this, we know that gratitude works on the resting amygdala allowing the brain to process and release tough emotions without any conscious work or recognition.

Let's bring this back to our PSNS and how gratitude can have a profound effect on this nervous system.

When gratitude is practiced properly, and the brain is in a state of gratitude, neurochemicals are released, and the vagus nerve signals the body to enter into a state of relaxation, or a parasympathetic state. In essence, our nervous system enters into a state of rest, breaking the fight or flight cycle we can find ourselves stuck in and allowing our mind and body to rest rather than perpetually preparing for the next attack.

A body that is in a parasympathetic state is a healthy body as deep sleep improves, metabolic functions work as they should, and the immune system begins to function correctly, lowering cortisol and boosting antibody production in the body. This, of course, reduces inflammation in the body leading to less pain and discomfort, and that cycle of inflammation and pain that we spoke about in Chapter 1 is broken.

After reading this chapter, I hope that the effects of gratitude are understood better and that you can see the importance of the practice and how it can change your body and brain long-term.

Neuroscience suggests that gratitude is not a modern human practice or some new-age self-help fad but rather an evolutionary emotion as old as humankind which has slowly been repressed as more conscious awareness has been placed on all of the things we lack rather than the things we have.

This makes sense when we think of the days of the hunter-gatherer who did not have the time to lament an escaped hunt or less than fruitful gathering. The human brain back then prioritized gratitude as a means of survival, motivating prehistoric humans to move on to the next possible successful opportunity to eat or sleep in safety.

What modern humans have taught us is that much of the danger we're exposed to, and the stress responses that follow, is perceived. A lot like the perception we have of all of the negative things in our lives.

It is remarkable to think that a shift in these perceptions can have such a profound effect on our lives and on our health, but science has proven that it does and that when practiced properly, gratitude is one of the oldest and most effective evolutionary tools we have for holistic well-being.

Chapter 3:
The Limitations and Negative Effects of Traditional Gratitude Practices

Gratitude, as a practice, is massively beneficial, but like most things in life, we need to know how to put its different aspects together properly. Baking a cake without both the ingredients and the instructions may produce something that looks like a cake, but it's never going to be an *actual* cake that can be used for its intended purposes if the right process isn't followed. If you were to be given some of the ingredients and directions, perhaps some people would produce something that resembles an edible cake once or twice, but how are they going to replicate their success or learn how to create the cake again without the proper direction? Gratitude is the cake of life, and self-help gurus are eagerly providing snippets of information and some ingredients while fervently declaring the now notorious saying, "Let them eat cake!"

The fact of the matter is that most self-help-style gratitude out on the market professes life-altering results based on an oversimplification of a process. I'm not claiming that gratitude is a complicated process—neither is baking a cake, for that matter—it's just that you're not being given all of the useful information you need to create a gratitude practice that changes your brain.

Gratitude is neither a quick fix nor is it a cure-all for everything life will throw at you or that has already used to smack you upside the head, but it is the key that unlocks the magical door to holistic well-being. Scratching the surface of self-help gratitude practices uncovers a multitude of issues with the information being disseminated to people like you and me.

We're taught to ignore our negative emotions, find something positive to fixate on, and write these things down. Ultimately we're left with lists and lists of things we should be thankful for, feeling terrible about ourselves because we're just not grateful for any of these things, or at the very least, are only grateful for some of them. It's a superficial, inauthentic practice that doesn't even begin to skim over genuine emotional engagement that actually resonates with our individual life experiences. This brings me to the next point.

Self-help brand gratitude places a strong emphasis on personal gratitude and the ego, or self. It doesn't address the environmental or societal issues or any of the other systemic hardships which contribute to our sadness or the state of humanity today. It's the equivalent of being grateful that our house isn't burning down while our entire neighborhood is on fire.

Now this is not entirely wrong. We have to change ourselves before we change the world, but there is an inherent danger in only focusing on ourselves and our own endeavors. That is, we risk stepping on the very humanity we claim we are grateful for as we pursue our own gratitude and inner joy. This kind of gratitude disregards our personal circumstances, rendering our experiences, struggles, and trauma completely irrelevant, and invalidates how far we've come as well as how far we have to go to achieve self-actualization. There is no balance in these practices, nor are they realistic, because on a fundamental level, they just don't work at changing anything other than slapping on a pair of blinkers and calling them rose-tinted glasses. The reality is that the world is not sunshine and roses, and most of us have some cross we carry around. Practicing self-help style gratitude tips the balance of this burden, making it harder to bear rather than easier.

In this chapter, I'll show you what obstacles may be encountered why traditional forms of gratitude can cause us emotional distress despite our best efforts in trying to find something that we can be thankful for in our lives. It's important that you know that by instituting these traditional practices we've done nothing wrong—traditional gratitude gurus are pretty convincing when they tell us it works! The issue is that these practices are not based in science, and that we run the risk of allowing our traditional gratitude practices becoming the very roadblock we're trying to overcome. We don't need to live a life that follows traditional gratitude, nor do we need to be limited by the obstacles of these practices. Instead, by using the protocol within this book, we can build effective gratitude practices that are easy to follow and that we can easily incorporate into our lives.

A. The Self-Help Gratitude Spiral: Invalidating Our Experiences and Emotions

One of the primary issues with guru-style self-help is that, by default, it invalidates an individual's experience of life. In creating a smokescreen around the things that have happened to us, we inadvertently place blame on ourselves, declaring we are the problem with everything life has thrown at us.

We've all heard the sentiment, "Bad things happen to us, it's what we do with those bad things that count." This statement is utter nonsense and suppresses not only the emotions we feel about our experiences but places a barrier between us and the processes needed to heal ourselves from our past. It creates stress, anxiety, and emotional dysregulation, all of which place the body and mind under enormous stress that we're trying to fix by saying to ourselves, "It's my fault this happened."

Counterintuitive, isn't it?

When we are told that the only way to be happy is to suppress our experiences and squash down how we feel, we begin to gaslight ourselves, wondering whether or not things are as bad as we make them out to be, and the beginning of a spiral of self-doubt and self-invalidation begins. We undermine our self-confidence, breaking the trust bond we have with ourselves as we minimize one experience after the next until, eventually, we're caught in a whirl of wondering what is wrong with us and why we have to work so hard to be grateful at all! Here's the issue with being gaslit: It diminishes our self-worth and sends the message that our perspectives, as well as how we feel, are wholly invalid. Self-acceptance and self-worth fly out the window, and we begin to seek validation from the outside world, placing strain on our relationships and inviting not-so-great people into our lives in an effort to find something, *anything* we can be grateful for.

It can become challenging to set personal boundaries or even recognize when our boundaries have been violated because we no longer believe in our own experience of the world, blaming ourselves for how others treat us. And, of course, this all suppresses our growth and healing. We never acknowledge or learn from our experiences, nor do we take the time to reflect so that we can develop the resilience we need to transform our circumstances. Instead, we become stuck in patterns of subconscious negativity while our conscious mind tells us all of this gratitude should work.

We cannot slap a Band-Aid on a gaping wound and expect not to bleed out (let alone heal from the wound), and since our experiences shape our emotions, self-help gratitude becomes the Band-Aid we're placing on our bleeding emotions. The thing is, the human mind is not designed this way—it *needs* to process emotions for it to heal and be healthy, and being dysregulated from our emotions is a recipe for disaster.

When we become emotionally dysregulated, we can no longer feel our emotions. This might sound great, especially if those emotions are ones of intense sadness or anger, but here's the thing about emotions: they demand to be felt. When we ignore them, they become more intense, last longer, and create unpredictability in how we will act in different situations. Our moods swing from a temporary high after writing our gratitude in our dedicated "gratitude journal," to a deep low the rest of the day, and the baseline we once had no longer exists.

In practicing improper gratitude, we create a situation in which we try to find the good while our mind fights to amplify the bad in an attempt for us to listen up and actually deal with the emotions we're having. And, instead of modulating our mood and our behaviors, we begin to act impulsively, placing more and more Band-Aids on our wounds until eventually, we're battling to survive, let alone communicate how we are feeling or what the problem was to begin with.

Neuroscience and psychology hypothesize that this is the reason so many people are walking through life with post-traumatic stress disorder (PTSD), why anxiety and stress are at an all-time high, and why people, in general, just don't know how to cope with life anymore.

For most of us, gratitude is already suppressed because of societal programming, and in further squashing down the other emotions we feel, we're compounding the problem. It's no wonder that with all the internal pain and the emotional storms brewing inside of us we would seek a quick fix, but it's important to remember that Band-Aids don't fix wounds.

1. *What Neuroscience Says About Guru-Style Gratitude*

I know all of this sounds very doom and gloom, and perhaps your inner cynic is already raising its hand to declare this to be yet another self-help book on gratitude, but there's a difference here. This book focuses on the science, not the promises of a mystical cure. It provides you with the ingredients and the directions to bake your gratitude cake and does so in a way that is simple enough to not only change the very structure of your brain but to turn the process of baking this cake—your gratitude practice—into an action that doesn't require much thought or attention.

Now, before we actually get into the nitty-gritty of how and why proper gratitude works, it's important to look at neuroscience's stance on the traditional guru-style gratitude and why it doesn't work in changing the brain.

Traditional gratitude practices simply don't lead to observable neurological changes because of the limitations of the methodology itself. Consistent, robust neurological changes only occur when gratitude is practiced correctly, and this can be attributed to two primary reasons.

Firstly, the practice of improper gratitude is often not sustainable. We spend so much time externally validating our existence that our brain simply doesn't see the value in what we are trying to do. Internally, we're still struggling, and our brain cannot understand why we insist on painting every pile of dog mess we come across with a slap of gold and pretending the putrid gunk is a gold nugget of some worth.

This brings me to the second reason, which is that we lack personal engagement in the practice of gratitude. We cannot engage with something we don't believe in on a deep, meaningful level. I mean, it doesn't matter how compelling and beautiful fantasy films are, we don't really believe that the characters of that film actually exist. On a fundamental level, we know it's all fantasy, and because of that, the multiple regions of our brains, along with the neurotransmitter systems involved in proper gratitude practices, don't engage. And all of this occurs because we live in a real world, not a fantasy one, and that means we are subjected to a whole lot of those piles of dog mess on a daily basis, and at some point, the gold paint runs out, doesn't it?

We dysregulate from our lives because it becomes too painful to admit that we're just not grateful for what that internet guru said we should be, and neuroscience proves it. Self-invalidation can disrupt regions of our brain, resulting in emotional dysregulation, increased stress responses, decreased sense of self-worth, and lowered neural plasticity (Powers et al., 2017). These areas of the brain include the prefrontal cortex, particularly the medial prefrontal cortex, the amygdala, the anterior cingulate cortex, the insula, and the hippocampus.

Now, if you were paying attention in the previous chapter, you will have noticed that many of the regions of the brain affected by proper gratitude are the same as those affected by self-invalidation. This means improper gratitude does the exact opposite of proper gratitude, hindering everything from our emotional intelligence to our ability to learn new skills and progress in life. In addition, improper gratitude directly affects the default mode of the network of our brain, preventing us from becoming truly introspective, altering our internal narrative, and causing ruminating thought patterns (Powers et al., 2017).

And all of this means we are not putting our proverbial money where our mouth is when it comes to traditional gratitude practices. The human brain is so incredibly complex that predicting the long-term outcomes of improper gratitude cannot be measured, but the amazing thing is that it's never too late to undo the damage caused.

2. *Improper Gratitude and the Nervous System: The Creation of Traumatic Invalidation*

Most of us will agree that some of the events that occur in the world are just plain extreme. We're exposed to acts of brutality, immorality, and chaos every day. Private opinions and attitudes form based on perception, and our brains filter this information, placing it in a space of indignation, agreement, or worse, neutrality. And these are only external events, some of which may hit close to home and others that neither affect our lives directly nor indirectly—they just exist in the realms of the planet we reside on. Our internal events and environment compound upon this external chaos, and most of us never heal from these.

Guru-style gratitude encourages this neutrality, sending a signal to the primal parts of our brains, letting us know that we haven't yet ascertained whether we're safe and valued in any given situation. The survival part of our brain, the area that triggers all of the stress mechanisms that help us escape danger, teeters on the precipice of imminent danger, and our bodies ready themselves to explode or implode in an attempt to save us from the monster that lurks in the darkness.

Self-invalidation is a form of trauma—it's a pervasive process that causes extreme harm not only to the brain but to the nervous system. It erodes at the walls of self-trust and all but destroys our commitment to love ourselves through all of the ups and downs of life. In essence, we betray ourselves on a fundamental level, refusing to accept our reality and disregarding the very thing designed to process our human experience and keep us safe. A dysregulated nervous system is a ticking timebomb of nuclear proportions. It solidifies a snowball effect that places the brain and nervous system into a downward spiral. The pervasive symptoms of PTSD, insomnia, depression, anxiety, and outright exhaustion, to name a few, set in, and the nervous system responds. But we invalidate these because traditional gratitude practices tell us that we should be grateful *despite* these symptoms. We don't understand our emotional outbursts, overreactions to our environment, or passivity to the atrocities of the world.

Over time, the HPA axis—the delicately balanced signals between our primitive brain, the amygdala, and our stress control center, the hypothalamus and pituitary gland, becomes dysregulated. Stress hormones flood our body as the adrenal glands release more and more chemicals into our body, begging us to process our experience, and the nervous system never concludes its intended cycle.

But why does it matter, and how does this affect us other than the insistent hum of anxiety, aggression, or depression?

When the nervous system is dysregulated, our brain begins to insist that past events, thoughts, and non-threatening behaviors are a threat source. Our bodies enter into a primitive cell-danger response, triggering our bodies to enter into defensive mode and remain there regardless of whether a threat has passed or not. This triggers neuroendocrine and inflammatory responses in our bodies, and ultimately, the cycle begins to deregulate the very physiological processes that keep us alive (Zielinski & Veilleux, 2018).

The average person on the street gives no thought to the biochemical factors involved in dysregulating our nervous system, and I guarantee you, neither does the self-help guru instructing you to ignore the psychological and physiological cues we're receiving. And, the issues we experience from being stuck in a cell-danger response are eagerly treated with pharmaceuticals that further invalidate our experiences, labeling us as unfixable products of the society we live in.

A dysregulated nervous system is a dangerous thing, it unbalances our lives in every aspect, destroys relationships, drives us to make poor life choices in a bid to balance stress hormones with their calming counterparts, all as we begin to live in chronic pain as inflammation wracks our bodies.

Invalidation in any form, whether by gratitude or not, is damaging. It instills a deep belief in us that what we are experiencing is neither reasonable nor significant, and our body and mind react, creating a storm of internal and external destruction.

We need to manage our emotional responses and behaviors, process them, and accept our life experiences to properly and positively alter our brain, calm our nervous system, and reteach our bodies to respond to our environment accordingly. Guru gratitude does none of this. It limits us, destroys emotional regulation, and sets us on a path to psychological and cellular destruction. It is a chronic, pervasive, and destructive form of emotional inhibition that has become a pretty significant indicator of psychological and physiological distress (Krause et al., 2003).

The real mystery of why traditional gratitude doesn't work is not as mysterious as it would seem though, and if these practices explained the *why, how,* and *what* of proper practice, we wouldn't so readily invalidate ourselves. We wouldn't live in a perpetual realm of ignoring the monsters under our bed, and instead, we'd put into practice neuroscience-backed gratitude that *does* alter our body and brain for the better.

And, with all of the knowledge provided, it's now time to get into the science-backed protocol of gratitude so that you can begin enjoying all of the benefits that come with proper gratitude practices on a psychological, physiological, and neurological level.

Chapter 4:
The Most Effective Gratitude Practice Backed By Neuroscience

Knowing why traditional forms of gratitude don't work is critical because it allows us to avoid behaviors and actions that "switch off" our neural circuitry. We know that traditional gratitude activates our defensive brain—the deep primitive parts that tell us to distance ourselves from something that just doesn't feel safe—because, on a fundamental level, we don't want to feel disassociated or dysregulated from our lives.

World-renowned, and sometimes controversial, psychologist Sigmund Freud boldly proclaimed that human beings exist in two states—the life drive and the death instinct. While this is a somewhat complex concept to unpack, it is important to keep in mind as these states are perhaps one of the first rudimentary references to the appetitive positive brain circuitry and our destructive aversive circuitry.

Freud stated that human beings defaulted to the death instinct through our learned behaviors, repetitive compulsions, and, you guessed it, disassociation. Now, the reasons for this death state are often extremely complex, but a common thread when examining this death instinct, or the defensive brain, is actually quite fascinating as it ties directly with our life drive or appetitive brain.

I know that psychology is not neuroscience, however, the two concepts go hand-in-hand because thoughts and the programming of these thoughts are what drive these two human states. We know that our death state is usually fueled by our basic need to belong and that the way out of the death state is to exhibit prosocial behaviors that allow us to fulfill this need to belong, it becomes far easier to grasp why the gratitude practices in this chapter work so well.

Allow me to solidify this point further. When we are young, we're taught that repressing our negative emotions is the way to fit in or bring us closer to the groups of people we choose to belong to. It's so deeply ingrained in us that repressing our negative emotions and experiences is the correct social behavior that well into adulthood, we perpetuate sayings like, "I don't want to be a downer," or we minimize what has happened with, "It's not a big deal."

Societal standards of communicating our experiences drive us into our death state, activating our defensive brain circuits, and then when we begin practicing traditional gratitude, we further minimize our experiences while still hoping to activate neurocircuitry that taps into our life drive.

It doesn't work—it can't because we need to tap into the primal parts of our brain that say, "Hey! We want more of this!" and since most people are not deliberately masochistic, our brains resist our attempts to solidify our death state. We need to be able to activate our prefrontal cortex so that our brain's evaluation and deeper thinking can give meaning or context to gratitude.

So what does work?

I'd like you to take a moment to think about the last time someone expressed gratitude to you, whether it was for something small like a "thank you" for the meal you'd prepared or something much larger like a promotion at work or recognition for a task you put a lot of effort into. It felt good, didn't it? Neuroscience shows that when we are thanked by someone else or when we observe instances of gratitude in other people, our prefrontal cortex engages, activating our appetitive circuits to rewire our thought processes and begin changing the brain for the positive. In other words, we need to be able to receive gratitude so that we can perceive it to be genuine. But that is still not the entire picture.

For the brain to engage effectively in just about anything in life, it needs to create its own narrative—it needs to create a story of our life that reinforces our core beliefs and affirms that we are reinforcing our prosocial behaviors so that we can continue to belong. In doing this, we release the neurochemicals required to connect our thoughts with our physiology so that we can create the required parallel pathways in our minds. When actively creating not only the physiological groundwork for change but also reinforcing this groundwork, we can rewire our default state from its programmed persistence of the pessimistic death force (Andrew Huberman, 2021).

We need a certain set of personal criteria to feel joyous in our lives, but we also need to work on these criteria, making them happen in a way that doesn't disillusion us or create a smoke and mirrors sense that everything is peachy when it's not.

A. Wired For Dark and Light: How Our Neural Circuitry Can Be Rewired

Neuroscience has studied the link between the psychological concept of light-dark and life-death instincts in our brains, and most neuroscientists are very familiar with how the brain is wired for external stimuli that reflect this concept. A great example of this is the human visual system which has similar parallel pathways to the brain.

The neurons in the human eye respond to stimuli, including light-receptive neurons that, when exposed to bright light, start firing at an exponential rate. Other neurons are designed to respond to darkness, and these neurons differ, are more plentiful, and are far more robust than those designed for light. It's theorized that these differences are a survival mechanism designed to keep us safe from what lurks in the darkness because human beings simply aren't designed to be nocturnal.

Our biological perception of the darkness, therefore, is that it's a much more scary place and for us to survive, we're required to respond with greater certainty to the blackness around us. What's important to note here is that darkness evokes a sense of fear, it's that "must survive" state, driven without much of a reward other than we have survived another day.

Having said that, light and the response to illumination also exist on a primal, biological level, but in terms of survival, the light comes with new opportunities to forage and hunt for sustenance—or at least it did when human beings couldn't pull into a drive-through. The fundamental difference from a neural circuitry point of view is that light comes with the tangible, satiating reward of sustenance in whatever form.

What neural circuitry teaches us is that human beings have the capacity for both dark and light, so to speak, but that the dark circuitry takes preference because it involves our very life, and if we're hungry, or need something outside of air, water, shelter, and food, it's not something that needs to be paid attention to immediately. What all of this means is that our brains prioritize the things that we *perceive* to keep us alive. Never forget, fear is a powerful driving force, one that our brains will keep us in until we have ascertained that nothing is going to snuff out our existence.

And look, it's not that we shouldn't pay attention to the dark because, as you know, invalidating these things is not a healthy state of being for anyone. But what we can do with proper gratitude practices is shift our minds to a more neutral state that tips the scales to a happier medium rather than swinging between two extremes. We do this with the help of the positive neurotransmitters that facilitate the activation of our reward systems.

And this is where neurochemistry comes in because the hormones, or chemicals produced in the body and brain, reinforce our perceptions of light and dark—appetitive and aversive—responses. It's these chemicals that are responsible for flipping the circuits in our brains and have the power to switch between the two extremes of death and life, as well as the ability to modulate ourselves at a specific midpoint mood.

The predisposition toward one of the extremes of appetitive or aversive affects the midpoint mood because the circuitry responsible for how we react to our environments is really well used, and more than likely has been solidified from a young age. It's a well-worn path in our brains that says this is the comfortable route to safety, and we default to it no matter how our environment changes.

In terms of the aversive brain, this path can be particularly stubborn to shut down even if we know it's an unsafe road to travel, and so we live our lives in the darkness, afraid of what the depths of this abyss holds for us. It doesn't have to be this way though. There are many people who are comfortable in the realms of darkness because they know that there's a high chance the darkness isn't as scary as it seems and know how to navigate themselves to the switch that turns on the light.

The metaphorical light switch for human beings is mostly serotonin which sends messages across different areas of the brain, telling our body to behave in a specific way to our environment. While dopamine certainly does play a role in solidifying prosocial behaviors, it's serotonin that begins the process of illumination.

Antonio Damasio is one of the most respected neuroscientists in the world and has dedicated his life to understanding how the consciousness of our brains creates biological and physiological reactions. He is a prolific advocator of emotional regulation and understanding the importance of emotions, as well as reframing our emotions from obstacles to gifts.

When studying the effects of gratitude, Damasio specifically looked at the two main areas of the brain affected by serotonin when respondents felt gratitude. Unlike most studies before this, the neuroscientist sought not only to uncover neural activity but also how different types of gratitude activated our brains. Using fMRI technology, Damasio and his team were able to gain astounding insights into the mechanics of the brain when respondents practiced neuroscience-backed gratitude.

Instead of expressing gratitude in the traditional sense of the word, respondents were asked to watch powerful stories of people experiencing positive things in their lives, specifically the stories of people who survived genocide. Remember, these respondents weren't the survivors, they were merely watching the narrative. These stories didn't gloss over the horrific tales of survival either but did include the characters and circumstances that helped the survivors from a physical and psychological perspective throughout their lives. The respondents in these studies showed robust, lasting activity in their brains but more specifically in the areas of the brain that display our affiliation with another person. In other words, the survivor's stories resonated with the respondents, and we know that the subjects of the study had never experienced genocide themselves. The study proved that we all feel that we are survivors on some level but also that giving gratitude is certainly nowhere near as powerful as receiving it because when we give gratitude, whether to ourselves or others, we're setting aside our own experiences to empathize with someone else's (Damasio & Carvalho, 2013).

Empathy, in itself, is a complicated emotion that requires us to set aside our own feelings and opinions about a situation so that we can see things from another person's perspective. Sure, empathy is a prosocial behavior too, but it's a temporary thing because we don't walk through life empathizing with everyone all of the time, and if we empathize with our own negative emotions all of the time, nothing would get done.

Now, before you tell me that not empathizing is the source of invalidation, you need to remember that empathy is designed to be temporary, and remaining in a state of empathy for what we feel without shifting to solutions-based thinking perpetuates the cycle of feeling sorry for ourselves. But this is a topic for an entirely different book.

What's important right now is that we have been handed all of the puzzle pieces of what powerful gratitude is—neural wiring, neurochemicals, narrative, and receiving of gratitude—and all that's left is to put these pieces together to form the bigger picture.

B. Highlighting the Differences Between Traditional and True Gratitude

We're already aware of the enormous benefits that come with proper gratitude practices, and if you need a refresher, head on back to Chapter 1. As a quick recap, proper gratitude reduces depression and anxiety, calms the nervous system, regulates heart rate, lowers blood pressure, and is just an all-around promoter of fantastic well-being.

Things like gratitude journals are nice to have but digging deep into the recesses of our memory to drag out five things we can write in our journal daily invalidates our life experiences and, quite frankly, just does nothing other than let our brain know that we're confused about our existence.

These traditional gratitude practices may temporarily activate the brain's neural circuitry, but it's nowhere near powerful or sustained enough to create the processes for sustained change. And, if traditional practices don't work in the way they're intended to, it only makes sense for us to find ways that properly engage our brains.

The human brain engages best in certain states, including repetition, patterns, and stories. There's a good reason that we're persistently on the hunt for a new series or character to love or hate. Great power lies in a great narrative and its ability to trick our brains into relating with even fictional characters in the most outlandish situations.

Our neural circuits light up when we hear or see other people's stories because storytelling is so deeply ingrained into the knowledge and memory centers of our brains. We retell stories we have heard or seen, in great detail, years after being exposed to them because stories are a language our brains understand.

Going back to Damasio's study, we can see that it wasn't only the brains of the respondents that engaged, but remarkably, listeners of the stories had their heartbeats synced, beating at the same rhythm, even when they were placed in different rooms. That's the power of storytelling!

Storytelling is the single most powerful tool in building the gratitude circuits in our brains, and activating gratitude through a story has the most potent effects on our ability to formulate not only a reframed perspective of our environments but also in being able to modulate our baseline mood.

I'm not saying you need to listen to horrific stories daily so that you identify with survivor stories, but you do need to reframe your own life into a story that you can tell yourself. This story needs to resonate with you and contain instances in which you have received gratitude, preferably when you observed genuine gratitude from someone meaningful in your life.

Why?

We want our neural circuitry to spark so that it gets itself into the gratitude emotion we have repressed for so many years. The more we practice this gratitude, repeating the story to ourselves, the quicker our brains will drop into its gratitude groove, so to speak, until this state becomes automatic.

Storytelling is such a powerful tool that studies outside of the renowned gratitude neuroscientist Andrew Huberman's investigations into these findings are being eagerly published and rehashed to further solidify this point.

One of these studies, conducted by Uri Hasson, a professor of psychology and neuroscience at Princeton University, showed that when a person is listening to a story, the brain responses of the storyteller and the listener are very similar (Hasson et al., 2018). Other studies by Hasson showed that the listeners' brain activity actively mirrored the storytellers in areas outside of the obvious language centers responsible for translating auditory cues in the brain.

Aside from the listener and storyteller connection, the brain engages when it creates stories, getting to work laying neural circuitry in the regions of the brain that evoke emotions, instill beliefs, and create the motivations or behaviors we need to place ourselves in this story. This is where storytelling becomes critical in the creation of proper gratitude.

We have already established that according to neuroscience, it appears as if gratitude is a long-repressed emotion or, at the very least, that gratitude acts as an emotion in our brains. In creating a story, we're activating the right areas of our brain to not only evoke a temporary emotion but to instill the beliefs that support the emotion and experience, and we begin to change our behaviors on a subconscious level to facilitate a life that celebrates gratitude.

Storytelling is an art as old as humankind and has been practiced through every stage of human evolution. Early information dissemination, moral teachings, and the actions learned for for prosocial behavior were all distributed through the stories people told and helped people make sense of the world and the tasks they needed to complete to both survive and fit in with other humans. Stories help us to make sense of the world and our experiences, and this perhaps explains why, when we invalidate our experiences, our brains spend hours, days, or even years playing the same scenario over and over again, formulating their own stories to solidify the very experiences we're trying to invalidate.

Storytelling has always been the one thing that is freely available to everyone as a way to communicate their experiences and the lessons they've learned. It's the most natural way to transfer information between people and within ourselves, and it inspires strong action. Our brains engage, ready to have our behaviors influenced by the story being told. Regardless of whether or not we believe we're storytellers, we are. It's ingrained in the biological programming of our brain and is a formidable tool just waiting to be unlocked for our greater good.

1. *The Art of Storytelling*

We now know why everyone loves a good story: The very design of our brain laps up the patterns, lessons, and imagery portrayed in narratives. We find characters to relate to, and our brain responds, changing behaviors that align us with these characters in the hopes that we will be rewarded with what they received. Writer and storyteller Vera Nazarian once said, "The world is shaped by two things—stories told and the memories they leave behind" (Nazarian, 2004), but many of us believe that storytelling is a complex art and talent bestowed on a few talented individuals.

The reality is that we all have storytelling inside of us, but some of us have never truly tapped into this area of our brain, choosing to focus on other abilities and talents. Storytelling is there though, in one of the back corner shelves of our minds, and it's really not that difficult to find it, dust it off, and tap into the incredible power of a compelling narrative.

If you're one of those people who feels that they lack the ability to create their own story of gratitude and that this means you'll never fully experience the powerful benefits of proper gratitude, allow me to take you through the steps needed to create your gratitude story.

Traditional storytelling begins with knowing our audience, and this is still true for us. We need to become introspective and figure out who we are and who we want to be on a fundamental level. Now, I don't mean that we need to go on a psychoanalytical hours-long tangent in which we uncover every facet of our lives, but we will need to set aside five minutes to figure out what is at our core.

Remember, we're creating a story about a time in which we received gratitude and it helps to solidify this gratitude with something we value in our lives. This means ascertaining who we are at our core without labels or the responsibilities we drown ourselves in as a way to separate ourselves from reality. We'll need to change our narrative from "I am a mother/father" to "I am a nurturer" or from "I am a salesperson" to "I am a compelling influencer of behavior."

The reason we want to tap into our intended "audience" is that we want to be able to speak about things we really care about. Our brains need to engage with a personal story that stimulates our intellect, emotions, and the things we find beautiful, familiar, and thought-provoking. Don't skim over this part because it's critical for the preparation of proper gratitude practices.

Ascertain what will set the scene by engaging the senses. This means knowing where this story takes place and recalling as many sensory details as possible. What does it smell like, what auditory and visual stimuli are present, who is present, and what did the moments leading up to the story feel like? This step should be completed before the chronology of the story or event.

Once we have taken down notes on all of the things that engaged our senses during this gratitude-receiving event, we can marry them up with chronology. There needs to be some context leading up to the act of receiving gratitude, and if we are to change our behaviors to ones that facilitate a life of gratitude, we need to figure out what we did to receive thanks in the first place. One of the easiest ways to recall memories of our behaviors and actions is to explore a scenario with curiosity and wonder. Think of receiving gratitude as puzzle pieces that need to be put in specific spaces for a bigger picture to form. Picking up these pieces, turning them over, and examining the patterns help us to work out where they go.

Now is the fun part, insert the instance of receiving gratitude into the story. When finding the gratitude sweet spot, it's important that we notice how we are feeling. A lot of the time, our brains will give us subtle, subconscious clues through our body language. We may catch ourselves smiling, our muscles relaxing, or we may even puff our chest out slightly. These changes in our bodies are sure-fire signs that our brain is engaged and actually enjoying the process of gratitude.

Finally, don't limit the experience once gratitude is felt. We need to solidify our experience by explaining how we felt, what behaviors changed for us, and why we believe we received this gratitude. This can be done by empathizing with the person giving us gratitude and asking ourselves how we helped them or how they must have felt when our behaviors were prosocial.

With all of these pieces now in place, we can begin to weave together our stories. Don't be limited by words or the need for the story to be perfect. What is important is that the narrative speaks to us, compelling our brains to recall the memory of receiving gratitude and solidifying our positive experiences. With all of the elements above in place, our stories will make us feel the way we did on the day of receiving gratitude, even if this feeling is not obvious to begin with. In creating our own gratitude stories, we activate the somatic circuitry in our brains, enhancing emotional regulation and calming our nervous systems. This, in turn, releases the right neurochemicals, stimulating the reward center of our brains and begins the process of positive neural development.

C. Creating Your Own Brain Changing Gratitude Practice

Professor of neuroscience and tenured associate professor in Neurobiology, Psychiatry, and Behavioral Sciences at Stanford University School of Medicine, Andrew D. Huberman, has been a solid contributor to the fields of brain plasticity, neural regeneration, and brain development. Recently, Huberman has turned his attention to the science of gratitude and the most effective way to practice gratitude for positive neural development.

While other neuroscientists have certainly researched and proven proper gratitude practices, it's the simplicity of Huberman's findings that we will use when creating your own step-by-step protocol for implementing proper gratitude in your life.

We have laid the foundation for effective gratitude practices by covering all of the information, and now we need to create a protocol that marries up all of the things we have learned with a sustainable practice that *doesn't* invalidate our experiences.

While creating your own gratitude protocol, it's important that you do so with consideration for your time. Practicing gratitude shouldn't feel like a chore, but rather something you're doing to improve your health and well-being. You never want to feel like you're settling or invalidating yourself. If you worked really hard and had to overcome struggles to receive gratitude, note this so that your brain understands that your resilience and persistence were an integral part of the gratitude process.

Proper gratitude practices will help you to feel good not just in the moment but afterward, perhaps not in a euphoric kind of way, but in a way that causes your baseline emotions to be calm and not anxious. Your gratitude practice is going to need some preparation and needs to be grounded in the story you create in which you received gratitude, *not* in instances where you have given thanks.

A key note here is that you do *not* need to recite your story verbatim. If reading is not something that appeals to you, why not try recording yourself telling your story so that you can play your story back to yourself while visualizing and replaying your story in your mind?

Your mind might need a little practice activating the right centers, and because of this, it's important that you're not throwing yourself into the deep end by trying to practice gratitude for a full five minutes. If you're finding that you're distracted, try reducing your gratitude time—anywhere between one and five minutes will work.

Finally, make sure that you recall a story that includes genuine thanks that you received. Once you are used to this form of gratitude, you can set aside the formal story creation part of the exercise, using a memory of a time when you received thanks. Or, if you really enjoy story creation, begin a journal in which you recall instances of gratitude in great detail so that you can choose which gratitude story you'd like to recall.

Here's a recap of the important aspects of proper gratitude practices.

- Don't invalidate your experience or emotions.
- Do recall as many details of your story as possible. Engaging all of your senses will help your brain to focus its attention on the moment you received gratitude.
- Stop to focus on keywords when you feel a surge of positive emotion.

- Take the time to remember how you felt after receiving gratitude.
- Don't brush over any other positive emotions when recalling this gratitude-receiving moment.
- You don't have to practice gratitude every day of the week. Three times a week is more than enough to feel the effects of proper gratitude without interfering with your schedule or making it feel like a chore.
- If you would like to continue to focus on things or people you're grateful for, only do so for 10 seconds per day.

We have a specifically designed gratitude protocol journal for you to support your practices and guide you when you need it. This is, of course, not mandatory, and you're welcome to use the checklist and quick guide in this chapter, but the journal can come in handy when you need a little extra direction. This journal can be found by simply typing in "Andrew Humington" and "The Neuroscience of Gratitude Journal" in your preferred search engine.

1. *Gratitude Isn't a One-Practice Deal*

Neuroscientists like Huberman, Dr. Brené Brown, and Antonio Damasio agree that gratitude for neural development is not a one-practice deal and that we need to incorporate gratitude into our lives in ways that validate our experiences while still acknowledging that we have a lot more than we think we do.

Gratitude is a *protocol*—a shift in mindset, in the same way that choosing to live a physically healthy lifestyle is. We need to make small but effective changes every day for us to actually feel the results of the protocols we put into place for our health and well-being.

I mean, sure! Going to the gym every day is going to do something for our health, but if we continue to eat unhealthily, smoke a pack of cigarettes a day, and chug gallons of coffee, our time in the gym isn't going to amount to very much, is it?

The same thing applies to gratitude—we have to incorporate it into as many areas of our lives as we possibly can. But here's where it becomes tricky. We don't want to fall into the same destructive gratitude patterns we were in before, and we certainly don't want to be in a position where we're digging up the neural pathways we are laying by chugging a metaphorical gallon of invalidating mumbo-jumbo.

So it's not just about creating a story in which you have received gratitude, it's a specific set of steps we need to take daily to reinforce our neural pathways and give us a boost of serotonin and dopamine so that we can experience a meaningful and long-lasting shit in our subconscious.

None of these activities are particularly time-consuming either, it's just that we've been taught that we need to set aside a specific amount of time to be grateful, and that in itself turns gratitude as a practice into somewhat of a time-waster for us. Think about it, those five minutes we're spending daily, dredging up daily to *find* things we're grateful for, amount to 35 minutes a week, two and a half hours per month, and more than one day of every year on an activity that simply doesn't work. And we know this on a subconscious level—that we're wasting our time and invalidating our experiences, so we begin to avoid traditional gratitude, eventually casting it aside and labeling ourselves as failures for not getting it right.

So what are these small changes that we need to make to form a solid gratitude protocol that works on a neurological level?

1. We need to move away from 5-minute appreciation tactics and focus on things we already have that we appreciate and that make our lives more enjoyable. This shouldn't last for more than 10 seconds and serves

purely as the trigger for setting off the neurochemicals we need to solidify our gratitude protocol. Think of these 10 seconds as a reverse adrenaline rush in which we are providing ourselves with a burst of joy and happiness rather than adrenaline. While this doesn't necessarily create neural pathways, it does stimulate the brain's reward center, making it more receptive to the other gratitude practices in our protocol.

2. We already know that receiving thanks is more effective than giving it, and this is the reason we create a gratitude-receiving story for our brains to engage with. A great way to sustain this gratitude-receiving effect is to express your own gratitude for others more often. In a study conducted by neuroscientists, respondents were to write letters of thanks to their coworkers. Each person was asked to read the letter they received out loud. The prefrontal cortex of the respondents responded strongly, reinforcing the notion that receiving gratitude has a much stronger effect than giving it (Hori et al., 2020). In order for us to receive more gratitude though, we need to express it more often. Don't worry, it won't be long before more gratitude will come your way!

3. Creating an atmosphere of gratitude is another extremely effective way to fire up our neural circuitry and release dopamine and serotonin. All that needs to be done is to select one area in your immediate surroundings that you associate with gratitude. Like almost every entrepreneur extraordinaire will tell you, the shower is their space to generate new ideas and spark inspiration, your gratitude atmosphere can be incorporated into just about anything you do or any space you're in, as long as it's consistent. Try incorporating gratitude walks into your week, create gratitude cooking and interweave it with mindfulness practices, or incorporate it into one of your other everyday activities. The point is not to set aside the rush or buzz of the day but rather to take a moment to

say, "Wow, I have the time to cook, even if it's just setting the microwave timer to 5 minutes."
4. Change out those podcasts from the same repetitive motivational messages you listen to every day and instead listen to stories of gratitude. Like the respondents who listened to the genocide survivor stories, listening to gratitude narratives will help fire up your brain, laying neural pathways for sustained change.
5. Finally, and this is a reiterated point, listen to your own gratitude story for between one and five minutes, three times a week to help solidify the neural circuitry being created.

Always remember gratitude protocols are not instantaneous, it takes time, small changes, and a willingness to change our mindsets without invalidating our experiences or our emotions.

If you've had a day that looks like something the dog brought up at breakfast, that's fine! Acknowledge and accept the moment for what it is and choose a quick 10-second gratitude focus session to give yourself a shot of dopamine and serotonin. Gratitude is not about ignoring the bad stuff that's happened, it's about understanding that everything is temporary if you don't allow your brain to live in the bad stuff permanently.

D. Your Gratitude Protocol Checklist

With all of the information you've been given in this chapter, it would be completely understandable if some of the more important aspects of your gratitude protocol slipped through the net. Don't worry, I've got you covered.

Below are tables designed to help you create your gratitude narrative and the steps that need to be taken for your protocol to begin working on a neurological level. You can tick these off, transfer them over to your gratitude journal, or even print them out so that you can tick each of these off and use them as a memory job.

While checklists and reminders are a great way to guide your practice, for those of you who don't want to have to print or copy this checklist, or who would like a more efficient way to create your gratitude protocol, we have a specifically designed gratitude journal for you. This can be found on Amazon by typing in my name "Andrew Humington" followed by "Gratitude Journal."

1. *Crafting Your Gratitude Narrative*

You're aware now that gratitude doesn't require you to journal things you're grateful for. Instead, we need to focus on the gratitude we have received or earned.

Here are the steps to crafting your gratitude narrative. Feel free to use the provided table or your gratitude journal to help in the creation process.

Step	Prompt	Response
Dig deep and recall a story in which you received gratitude.	I was thanked for…	
Recall this memory in as much detail as you possibly can.	Who thanked me, where were we, what led up to being thanked, details I remember are…	

Tap into your emotions. Be vivid with how you felt and include non-verbal responses.	I felt... when I was thanked. I remember... My body responded by... My emotions were...	
Establish the reasons why this gratitude was so meaningful to you.	Being thanked for my behaviors/actions made me feel incredible because...	

If you cannot think of your own gratitude story, that's fine, by practicing this gratitude protocol, you'll begin to receive gratitude more often because it promotes prosocial behaviors. In the meantime, you can create a gratitude narrative about a situation in which someone else received gratitude, even if it's fictional. As long as you are deeply moved by this act, and you can remember it in great detail, it will work!

Once you have your gratitude narrative in place, it's time to actually get to your gratitude practice. Remember to institute this protocol into your current routines and habits so that you don't succumb to the "no time" excuse.

Step	**Cue**	**Response**
Tune into your emotion, paying attention to how you feel. Acknowledge these emotions and write them down or say them	I am feeling... The emotion I am feeling is... These feelings are important to me because...	

out loud.		
Get your nervous system involved. Make sure you have a pen on hand or make an electronic note because these will become your cues so that you don't have to recall your entire story every time you practice gratitude.	Cue word 1 Cue word 2 Cue word 3 Cue word 4 Cue word 5 Cue word 6 Cue word 7 Cue word 8 Cue word 9	
Intentional reward acknowledgment. This can be how you are feeling right now or how your future baseline emotions will be affected by your gratitude practices.	I feel great because... I am calm because... My emotions right now are... I accept my content state because...	

Both of these tables will help you to create your gratitude protocol, instituting it into your everyday life. Remember to add your 10-second dopamine boost when you feel a slump and to practice mindfulness and acceptance as you embark upon your journey to a grateful life.

If you need a little additional help and a reminder, feel free to use the table below as a checklist and a visual tool that helps you see when you've practiced gratitude, mindfulness, and acceptance.

Practice	Week	M	T	W	T	F	S	S
Gratitude narrative	1							
10-second dopamine boost								
Mindfulness								
Acceptance								
Gratitude narrative	2							
10-second dopamine boost								
Mindfulness								
Acceptance								
Gratitude narrative	3							
10-second dopamine boost								
Mindfulness								
Acceptance								
Gratitude narrative	4							

10-second dopamine boost							
Mindfulness							
Acceptance							

Now I know I told you that you don't need to practice your gratitude protocol every day, but in the beginning phases of your journey, I do suggest trying to incorporate it into your daily routine until you've established good habits. Consistency is key, and you need to give your brain the best possible opportunity to begin creating new neural pathways and to learn how to reward itself with positive neurochemicals.

Always remember that there are no quick fixes in life and no one-size-fits-all approach to anything. Anything worth achieving in life is a lifelong endeavor that is going to require commitment, patience, and the ability to become introspective in tough times. May you enjoy this journey to gratitude, stop to celebrate your victories often, and take the time to acknowledge just how far you've come without ever fearing how far you have to go.

And now it's time for you to take a deep breath, grab your gratitude journal, and wave goodbye to negativity as you embark upon this voyage toward contentment and joy.

Chapter 5:
Overcoming Barriers to Gratitude Practice

Knowing the reasons why we practice gratitude is great, and it certainly provides most of us with that initial boost of motivation we need to be able to institute our gratitude practices. Here's the thing, motivation is temporary, and it will need to give way to self-discipline if we are to succeed in whatever it is we want.

Every single one of us is going to hit some form of a barrier when it comes to our gratitude practices and a lot of these barriers begin in our brains on a psychological level. Now I know, "I don't have enough time," seems like a valid excuse, but here's the thing, we always carve out time for the things that are a priority in our lives. So what exactly is it that drives us to put up these barriers when it comes to our gratitude protocol?

Let's begin with our excuses. These are the things we tell ourselves are the reason we're not practicing gratitude.

- I forgot because there's too much on my schedule.
- I simply don't have the time.
- I'm skeptical about whether this will work or not.
- It's been a week, and I feel no different.
- I really don't feel sincere when I do this.
- I feel guilty for taking the time to be grateful.
- I'm going through a really tough time, and there's not much to be grateful for.

These are all excuses and are not the real reasons we are not practicing gratitude. Here's the thing about life, it's a series of decisions we need to make and ultimately it boils down to one choice—to act or not to act.

I'm not saying we make the choice not to act on a conscious level, although some people do, but for the most part, choosing to not take action is a result of subconscious processes and thoughts going on in our brains.

In essence, our brains are hijacking our motivation to act because of a set of biases and beliefs we hold as a result of the negative bias circuitry that we've built. If we break it down, this negative circuitry consists of our inner critic, biases, self-limiting beliefs, and being bombarded with images of what success looks like, creating comparison tendencies.

From an external influence point of view, life does throw challenges our way, and I'm not saying that there won't be days when we simply cannot carve out the time to be grateful as we take a 2-minute splash and dash shower before collapsing into bed at midnight in the hopes we'll get anywhere near enough sleep, it's just that those days are generally few and far between.

Those manic days aside, we have to develop a deeper understanding of why we are self-sabotaging our gratitude protocols in a way that is both honest and non-judgmental. On a fundamental level, we need to learn that absolutely nothing in life is perfect and that the essence of life is progression, not perfection. Knowing that the obstacles we're placing in our own paths are occurring on a psychological and neurological level helps us to understand that the common barriers we face can be overcome with a little bit of mindfulness and a lot of self-awareness.

With that in mind, it's important to label these self-made obstacles, and when it comes down to it, the most common of these are expectation, comparison, and negativity bias. You'll notice that "not having time" is not on this list, and for good reason! If you have time to scroll through social media, stream an episode of your favorite show, commute to work with your earbuds in, shower daily, or cook one meal a week, then you have the time. The nature of proper gratitude is not that we need to set aside time but that gratitude is incorporated into our time.

At the root of our avoidance is the fear that our lives may become better, that things will change, and that if they change, we will be forced to be comfortably happy rather than comfortably unhappy. Human beings don't crave change, we crave stability, and if we're stable in our own misery, our brains feel safe. We form expectations about everything in our lives about how things should unfold, what the outcome should be, and how others should act, and when this *should* variable is removed from our narrative, our brains become fearful replacing the *shoulds* with *what ifs*.

"What if it doesn't work and I need to face the remainder of my life like this," or "What if it does work and people don't accept the new me?" We begin to play every outcome over and over again in our minds, fixating on the negative and never stopping to reframe these thoughts to, "What if it works and I have a life filled with joy?" And this is not our fault, our brains are wired for safety, certainty, and familiarity. We're programmed with the belief that the *unknown* is a bad and scary thing, even if our certainty is causing us to live a life that is less than it should be.

Most of our biases revolve around the long-programmed beliefs our parents and other people instilled into us when our brains were young and impressionable. We're taught there is a standard of what success looks like, and this is further solidified by social media which fuels our emotional patterns and negative biases by telling us we're not successful if we don't attain unreasonable standards. We're not taught to question things, and as such, we never ask ourselves how we define success for ourselves. We don't see success as something that is as unique and as malleable as we are and begin to compare our lives to that of others.

We begin to form a void inside of us in which we operate on autopilot, chasing other people's dreams and standards, and when something, like gratitude, comes along, we expect it to fill this void while still operating on our negatively-biased autopilot. Western cultural influences further solidify that, on some level, misery and suffering is our default state of life, and we're brought up with common sayings like, "Life is hard, and then you die," or "No one really cares about how you feel, suck it up!"

And all of this outward programming and listening to our negative biases and inner critic just compound our excuses while we build on the barriers that prevent us from the benefits of gratitude.

Before I get into how we can become more self-aware of these biases and how to overcome our *what-ifs* and *shoulds*, it's important to take a look at the neuroscience behind the ungrateful brain. Only once we understand *why* our brains do what they do to keep us in a comfortably uncomfortable state can we switch off the autopilot and truly embrace gratitude as an essential protocol in our lives.

A. The Ungrateful Brain

Research shows that a brain that is not trained for gratitude has some neurological and structural differences from the grateful brain. People who have incorporated gratitude protocols into their lives have more gray matter, specifically in their right inferior temporal cortices, which directly affects their ability to interpret people's intentions and emotions (Zahn et al., 2013). People who are inclined to make excuses or drop their gratitude practices have lower function in the brain regions that process moral cognition, perspective-taking, and even the reward center (Fox, 2017). In addition, people who practiced gratitude and mindfulness techniques had a brain that was more active when making decisions, mentally calculating their environment, and processing perceptions (Karns et al., 2017).

All of these studies conducted into the grateful brain show that the reward center of the people who practiced proper gratitude protocols was far more active and receptive to dopamine and serotonin production, solidifying the good behaviors associated with gratitude as a practice. What's critical to understand here is that neural structure can be changed because the brain exhibits plasticity. Our neural circuitry is not static, but it does enjoy familiarity because it helps us automate more processes. This is good news because it means we have a choice to shift our ungrateful brain to a grateful one, but we will first need to become aware of our biases, inner critic, and self-limiting beliefs.

Now, research shows that proper gratitude practices do change the brain's structure and lays new neural circuitry. In fact, 38 gratitude studies conducted in 2017 showed that intervening in the processes of the ungrateful brain created a profound shift in all respondents in terms of their baseline emotions, their satisfaction in life, their well-being, and their general disposition. So the real question is, how do we shift the ungrateful brain to a grateful one in a way that we don't "forget" about our gratitude protocol or get stuck in our excuses?

We have to become self-aware first and foremost, and that means becoming more mindful of our thoughts and biases. This is not the easiest thing to do though, and we may need to employ some trusted people in our lives to help us identify when we're limiting our forward movement or are operating in our negative bias default state of mind, especially when we live so much of our lives in autopilot.

I'd like you to take a minute to recall Freud's theories on life and death instincts and how we, as people, have a tendency to live within this death instinct. This doesn't mean we want to literally die, but it does mean that our brain is going to try to switch to a default state of fear and uncertainty as a survival mechanism, especially when facing new or uncomfortable situations. We need to understand that it doesn't always have to be that way. The monster in the dark does disappear when we switch on the lights, and in our mind, the lights are the information and tools we receive to help bring attention to the thoughts and behaviors that limit us.

Before reading the section below, I'd like you to take a moment to acknowledge that your body and mind are marvelous creations that are designed to be malleable and to grow and change. Uncertainty is scary, sure, but without getting up, falling down, and getting up again, we would never have learned some of the most crucial skills of our lives.

B. Enhancing Self-Awareness Through Mindfulness Practices

Mindfulness and self-awareness have been mentioned a few times throughout the previous chapters, and while a couple of people may not know what it truly means to be mindful, many of us think of mindfulness as meditation practices.

Now, this assumption isn't wholly incorrect, but we do not need to isolate ourselves, sitting in a pretzel-esque position, chanting, "Om" to practice mindfulness. Meditation requires mindfulness, but we don't need to meditate to be mindful or to reap the benefits of becoming more self-aware.

The benefits of being mindful are pretty widely known, but most of these benefits surround the psychology behind mindfulness and its ability to help us cope with the symptoms of depression, and stress, and in finding our purpose in life. Of course, there's nothing wrong with looking at the psychological benefits of any practice, but psychology only really makes sense when we back it up with neuroscience.

When we explore the science as well as the theoretical aspects behind the practice we can make sense of it and provide ourselves with a reason for wanting to become mindful and, at the same time, know what mindfulness is doing for us on a physiological level. With that in mind, let's examine the origins of mindfulness as well as the theoretical and science-based effects of the practice and how they can enhance our gratitude protocol.

Mindfulness first appears in history in Buddhist texts and translates to "clear comprehension." Throughout history, mindfulness has been used to help people shed their judgments and comprehend our environment more clearly so that we can respond, not react, in the proper way to the ups and downs of life. When we are able to respond rather than react, we begin to operate from our wise minds, and this means we make good choices rather than ones based on emotion or too much rational thought. Mindfulness encompasses gratitude and compassion, but that doesn't mean that it is a gratitude practice—we can be grateful without mindfulness, but we cannot be mindful without gratitude. It's the art of being able to notice our emotions without judgment, accept our thoughts without criticism, and acknowledge that both of these are merely fleeting moments in time.

All of this, of course, is theoretical and anecdotal, but neuroscience proves that mindfulness works to positively influence and change different areas of our brains on a structural level. It affects our ability to pay attention, become self-aware, and regulate our emotions, as well as positively influence the function of our brains. Neuroplasticity increases as new neural connections are formed as well as the pathways for emotion, attention, and self-awareness become stronger. And, the default mode network (DMN) of the brain—the area that controls the brain when it is at rest—decreases rumination and improves actual rest without being focused on the external environment and stimuli (Tang & Leve, 2016).

Using fMRI technology, neuroscientists have been able to uncover what areas of the brain mindfulness works on, not just temporarily, but with sustained practice, in long-term structural changes. Unsurprisingly, these changes don't only positively affect the brain but the nervous and neuroendocrine systems, lowering stress hormones and our body and helping to modulate the hypothalamic-pituitary-adrenal (HPA) axis. So where does mindfulness work, and how does it correlate with fMRI studies conducted into gratitude?

Mindfulness has been shown to strengthen activity within the prefrontal cortex, which dominates our executive functions like self-regulation, attention span, and decision-making. It also activates the dorsolateral prefrontal cortex that is responsible for modulating and calling on attention span, as well as the ventromedial prefrontal cortex that controls our ability to be self-aware and regulate our emotions. The anterior cingulate cortex, which helps to regulate our attention control and monitor conflict, is enhanced by mindfulness, allowing us to improve our attention span as well as our reactivity to negative environmental stimuli.

Within the insula, our awareness of our bodily sensations and our internal state improves, allowing us to become non-judgmental on a subconscious level and heightening our awareness of our internal experiences so that we can proactively change things that don't promote positivity and forward movement in our lives. Mindfulness also solidifies increased gray matter within the hippocampus, increasing the density of the gray matter produced through gratitude protocols.

Finally, within the posterior cingulate cortex (PCC), self-referential thinking, or self-awareness, decreases. This is a good thing because it means our mind spends less time in those *what-ifs* and more time in the present moment. As a result of this activity in the brain, neuroplasticity increases over time, which is excellent. Our ability to learn, grow, and unlearn means that we can shed ourselves of our ungrateful brain so that we can begin to live a life that is filled with contentment, happiness, and purpose (Schuman-Olivier et al., 2020).

Marrying up mindfulness and gratitude may seem like a natural process but it can take a little bit of effort on our part. You see, with mindfulness you need to be able to set an intention, train our minds to pay attention, and actively shift our attitude to one that embraces both compassion and curiosity. Here's the good news about mindfulness, it doesn't take long to begin working on a physiological level, and some reports show that with proper practice, as few as five short sessions of mindfulness will begin the process of calming the central and autonomic systems. Within a month of proper mindfulness practices, our brains begin to change on a physiological level, solidifying the progress we have made with our gratitude protocols.

From a psychological perspective, mindfulness helps us to identify the negative thought patterns and biases we have developed and to step outside of these so that we don't react or begin to ruminate about what is going on in our heads. The issue with rumination is that it triggers us, flipping the switch on unhappy memories, and forcing us to live in the past, or worse, a doomed future in which we repeat our mistakes. By training our brains to be mindful, we're able to flip this switch off, pausing for a moment from a state of, "I should," to just being present in the moment.

Here's the thing about gratitude, no matter how often we practice it, if we're not being mindful of our thoughts, we're going to become triggered and ultimately be swallowed up by our negative biases and deeply repressed anger. Even if this happens on a subconscious level, our brains are going to know that our gratitude is superficial and the new neural circuits we're trying to build are never going to take. Mindfulness brings our subconscious to the conscious and helps us to deal with our emotions in a constructive way so that we free up the space for our neural gratitude circuitry. In addition, being mindful provides us with insight so that we can spot the moments we're being triggered before we enter into a thought spiral and begin drowning in our negative emotions. This allows us to avoid reinforcing rumination and encourages our brain to focus on what matters—gratitude.

We can learn to become aware of our thoughts and become active participants in our own lives so that we no longer feel like life is happening to us. When we do this... when we are truly present, we can begin to spiral into positivity, not negativity. We can consciously learn to dial down our stress responses and choose to change our reactivity to activity, or even no action at all. That is the beauty of mindfulness: It acknowledges the fleetingness of life and all its moments without instilling fear or panic. Instead, it fills us with wonder and curiosity and an insatiable need to enjoy the time we have on this planet.

All of this is not science fiction. It lies in our brain's ability to change the activity of different regions and, more specifically, its ability to learn how to regulate our emotions and become resilient to stress. On a fundamental level, a positively changed brain rewards itself with neurochemicals that drive our body to behave in a conscious or subconscious way that facilitates more positive change.

The benefits of mindfulness have been recorded by proper scientific research, both on a psychological and physiological level. And because mindfulness activates so many similar areas of our brains associated with gratitude, it makes sense that we use mindfulness as a way to *enhance* our gratitude protocols. Mindfulness as a standalone tool is great, and I am in no way lessening its power, but when we combine it with gratitude, something truly powerful begins to happen in our brains—an unstoppable upward spiral toward self-actualization, purpose, and inner joy.

1. Non-Judgment in the Face of Negativity

Being judgmental is not great, and a lot of us have at least tried to become less judgmental of others and their circumstances at some point in our lives. Using judgment and being judgmental are not the same thing though, and judgment is actually something we have to do every single day—it's just the way our brains work. This action is the shortcut that occurs in our brains, and it allows us to process a whole lot of information in split seconds. For the purposes of this section, I'm going to use the phrase "weighing" to refer to our brain's ability to judge, just until it's easier to understand the difference between judgment and judging in terms of what our brain's function is.

When our brain weighs in on all of the information it receives, it eliminates unsafe or non-useful options based on past experience, knowledge, bias, and so on. Let's take street crossing as an example. We're taught to look both ways and back again before we cross any street. In the beginning, this was a conscious action that eventually becomes second nature. While crossing the street, our brains weigh whether or not traffic is coming, what the distance of this traffic is, and whether we can safely cross the street. All of this happens mostly without thought, including the involuntary action of actually walking across the street. In other words, our brains judge the safety of the action we're about to take.

Right, so while we're waiting to cross the street, someone drives past us, and for whatever reason we decide we don't like their face, or the car they're driving, the music they're listening to, or whatever. We consciously begin to have thoughts that criticize that person, creating scenarios in our heads in which they're one of the villains in the story of our lives. Alternatively, we notice an elderly lady beside us and decide she's wonderful and she becomes someone who needs saving, or whatever the scenario plays out in our heads. This is judging—a subconscious act based on our presumptions, beliefs, and biases that become conscious thoughts we ruminate on.

But, what if the person driving past us is a really great gal or guy who gives back to the community, works hard, and is the hero, and the elderly lady has a literal closet full of skeletons? You see, judgment doesn't serve a purpose other than to reinforce our limiting beliefs, cognitive distortions, and biases whereas to weigh, or judge, is designed to keep us safe. Even non-judgmental people judge, if they didn't they wouldn't be safe, but they do not pass judgment on others or themselves.

Here's the issue with being judgmental and reinforcing all of the things we believe are bad in our lives—it is often turned on ourselves. Our inner critic has a field day passing the same commentary on ourselves as it does on the other people we're judgmental toward. In fact, a lot of the time this commentary is far harsher when it is directed inward because so many of us are unaware of how much bias we carry around with us all of the time. And every time we entertain our inner critic, we reinforce our cognitive distortions, driving home the point that the people we compare ourselves to are the heroes and we are villains in our own story.

Okay, now we know the difference between judging and being judgmental—judging is a shortcut in our brains designed to make safe decisions, and being judgmental is assigning an opinion, good or bad, to a person, object, or environment. Judgment creates a thought process that is negative or positive—"Wow, this flower is absolutely stunning," or "Ug, this flower is the worst color!" while judging is simply acknowledging that the flower exists, "This is a flower."

Mindfulness is the ability to operate outside of judgment, whether internal or external and to understand that acknowledgment and judgment are two different constructs. Of course, this doesn't mean having to give up on complimenting others or ourselves, nor does it mean that we don't see the beauty around us, but we do need to give up the notion that things are either good or bad. There's a whole world of color between our judgments and it's up to us to train our brains into seeing the world in technicolor.

Ironically, the five senses we possess are what guide our ability to judge the safety of a situation but we neglect to use these senses when forming judgment. We either see or hear something and instantly default to whatever our cognitive distortions are because we don't acknowledge the very existence of whatever it is we're in judgment of. And here's the thing about distortions, they're based in thought—it's our thinking, not our brains that are generating this judgment. If we allow our brains to do what they're designed to do—keep us safe, and explore the world with curiosity and wonder—we begin to free ourselves from the negativity that pervades our lives.

We need to understand that we can feel a certain way about our behaviors or where we are in our lives without assigning our behaviors to who we are as people. Ultimately, it comes down to our intent, and aligning our values with the intent. In becoming aware of the fact that our minds are programmed, and certainly reprogrammable, we can begin to understand that our intentions are not to harm or hurt others or ourselves but that we simply need to reboot our brain's systems, writing new metaphorical code so that we can begin to operate in a more natural state of mind. Mindfulness is this code and gratitude is the hardware.

C. Neuroscience-Backed Mindfulness

Much of neuroscience relies on our ability to identify when we are experiencing subconscious or programmed behaviors and thoughts. This means we need to actually start to catch ourselves when we begin to judge ourselves and others. For us to gain a better perspective on the negative things that happen in our lives we first need to know that there is a chance our thoughts are exaggerating, or at the very least, extending our misery and discomfort.

This doesn't mean we invalidate our experience, but we do need to acknowledge that a bad thing only affects us for a certain period of time and that it's our thoughts and biases that create our extended experiences of agony, anger, and so on. Here's the thing, it's our judgment that has us framing our situations as bad in the first place. Now, I'm not saying that life isn't fraught with obstacles or that horrific things never happen. Mindfulness doesn't strip us of our experiences, it simply helps us to accept these experiences and come to terms with the thoughts and feelings we have about them. So the very first step in becoming mindful is actually catching ourselves in the act so-to-speak.

While this is how we develop self-awareness, we also need to be cognitive of the fact that judgment is both positive and negative. We need to be able to notice *all* of our judgments, regardless of how we are perceiving our environment and the people within it. I mean, what we might deem to be a funny light-hearted moment could be extremely offensive to someone else—it all revolves around perception.

Now comes the tricky part. How does our brain moves to solidify its neural pathways? We begin to justify our judgment by judging it! Think about it, how many times have you done something that has annoyed you? Let's say you drop a glass, it shatters and we begin to form a judgment, "You're so clumsy! What is wrong with you?" and then instead of just accepting that the glass is broken, the brain begins to ruminate and solidify what has happened, "Look at this glass. You've made so much work for yourself. It's because you don't pay attention. It's not clumsiness, it's stupidity. You're so stupid. You need to learn to pay more attention to what you're doing..." and the spiral of judgment upon judgment upon judgment begins. We need to be able to stop in those moments and observe our thoughts so that we can pick these judgments out because it's these judgments that often uncover our biases and cognitive distortions as well as our self-limiting beliefs.

Once we have identified these thought patterns we can either choose to accept them or challenge them so that we can change our subconscious thought patterns. In other words, we need to consciously begin to dig up the old neural pathways so that we can begin to lay the new positive ones. Cognitive restructuring fires the right areas of our brains, and when we engage these areas of the brain we are effectively intervening in our dysfunctional thought processes so that we can replace them with adaptive ones (Crum, 2021). In other words, we're not invalidating our experiences, we're simply reframing them.

It really is that simple when we put the concept to paper but in practice, it takes time and effort. Cognitive distortions and biases are those pesky oil stains that require persistent and specific methods to clean. We cannot hope to change our neural structures and circuitry if we continue to allow our brains to ruminate on the thoughts that formed our neural circuitry, to begin with.

A great way to do this is to take a few minutes every day to begin describing objects around you without judgment. This allows you to practice mindfulness, bringing your subconscious thought processes into the conscious mind. Here's an example: "This is a fork. It's used to bring food to my mouth easily. It is silver, cool to the touch, and it has blunt points."

Be specific about what you're describing, using facts and specifics without bringing emotion into the equation at all. One thing we need to be aware of is that judgment is ingrained in us. For us to be able to overcome the obstacles that come with gratitude we need to be able to accept that our brains are programmed in a certain way. By doing this we declutter our minds, freeing ourselves of our assumptions about our environment, and freeing up space for our gratitude practices.

As human beings, we are wired to hear stories and interpret them in a way in which we are either the hero, the victim, or the villain. But, stories are often full of assumptions, and it's these assumptions that affect whether or not we can practice gratitude with the right story that engages our brains.

Here's the thing about obstacles and barriers, they're not impermeable, never-ending sources of frustration if we don't allow them to be. We can move around them, over them, and even through them if we allow our minds to let go of seeing the obstacle and instead, see the bigger picture. If it's a mountain we need to overcome, there are ways around it. We don't need to give up or insist that we exhaust ourselves every step of the way. We can learn to embrace the journey through mindfulness and accept that most of life is simply putting one foot in front of the other while we either enjoy the view.

Chapter 6:
Making Gratitude a Long-Term Habit

Habits may feel like they are formed overnight but they're not and it take a couple of key elements for them to become solidified in our minds, creating automatic behaviors. Before we continue with this chapter, I'd like to make one point clear—habits can be both good and bad.

A lot of the time, we associate habitual behavior with all of the things we're doing that aren't great for our well-being, but the reality is that anything we do automatically is a habit. Added to this, our brains cannot differentiate between good and bad habits, it simply processes the information based on repetitive, routine actions and thoughts. Neuroscience and psychology have examined habit formation in depth and have shown that we never truly "break" habits. Now, don't panic, that doesn't mean we cannot rid ourselves of poor behaviors, it just means that we need to form a new habit with new neural circuitry that is stronger than our old habits. But here's the tricky part: Our habit formation requires a reward that is going to solidify our behavior. Because we're unique individuals, a reward may mean something totally different for each of us, but more on that later. For now, let's look at the areas of the brain that are involved in habit formation.

Within the basal ganglia, our dorsolateral striatum and sensorimotor striatum need to be activated for habitual behaviors to form. This interconnected structure is buried deep within our brain and receives messages from both our cortex and our thalamus, which will help our behaviors become automated. This means we also need to engage our prefrontal, orbitofrontal, and dorsolateral prefrontal cortexes. While these areas of our cortex are not activated once a habit is formed, they are necessary for the early phases of habit formation because they encode our cue responses while evaluating how we will be rewarded for our behavior.

The hippocampus, which is responsible for learning and memory formation, is also crucial for early habit formation because it helps to solidify the information received from our behaviors. Once a habit becomes an automatic behavior, the hippocampus is less involved, handing over the responsibility of carrying on with the habit to our basal ganglia. Incidentally, the dorsal striatum, a part of the basal ganglia, is instrumental in solidifying and perpetuating habits. It receives the cues required to begin behaviors, responds, and triggers the rewarding process, reinforcing and establishing the neural connections we need to turn actions into habits.

The cerebellum and amygdala are also heavily involved in habit formation as these areas of our brain fine-tune our motor coordination and behaviors when creating a habit and process the emotions we feel once we have created a habit, respectively. When we experience negative emotions, we're less likely to form a habit, and if we experience positive emotions, we are more likely to create and reinforce habits.

What's really important to remember when we form a habit is that our brains are really complex and require us to both execute and reinforce our behaviors and actions for a habit to form. In addition, our personal preferences can weigh heavily on whether or not our behaviors will form a habit—I mean, if you really dislike Brussels sprouts, chances are you're not going to create a habit of eating them unless there's a pretty substantial reward for doing so.

So what is the best way to form a habit, according to neuroscience?

A habit loop is the process of creating a habit, and I'll let you know how this works a little later in this chapter, but we need to know what the components of a habit loop are before we dive into it. For a habit to form effectively, our brain requires us to make a conscious effort to create a behavior. This means consistently repeating behaviors or actions and overcoming obstacles until we reach a desired behavior. It's this consistency in our behaviors that creates and strengthens neural connections over time, making it more automatic as it becomes ingrained over time. We also need to create a conscious habit loop—I'll explain this in the next section—so that our brains are able to recognize a cue, respond to it, and reward themselves for the behavior.

The context of our behaviors as well as the environment we're in, also plays a very important role in creating a habit, as our brains like to work in both a familiar environment as well as within the patterns we have already formed. Coincidentally, replacing a bad habit is far easier in an unfamiliar environment because our brains are too busy trying to create new patterns of familiarity to worry about a habit. This is the reason most people are able to kick bad habits when they're on vacation or when they move.

Once we have consciously completed the actions that we want to become a habit, we need to reinforce these behaviors with positive emotions so that we can facilitate the release of dopamine and activate the reward and motivation centers of the brain. The reward will increase the chances that the behavior will be repeated so that the brain can get a much-needed fix of dopamine again. Finally, we need to be patient but persistent in our efforts to form a habit. Small steps toward our end goal are far easier to achieve and increase the likelihood that we will activate the reward center of our brains, and as we build upon these small actions, we begin to create a repetitive pattern that ultimately forms a habit. The good news is that it doesn't take long to form a habit, and (with the proper steps in place) in as little as 59 days, you could be habitually practicing gratitude for a happier life.

The Habit Loop Explained

Pulitzer-prize winning author and reporter, Charles Duhigg, first simplified how habits are formed in his book, The Power of Habit. By examining the neuroscience and psychology behind habit formation, Duhigg was able to break habit formation down into an easy-to-understand three-step process. This process uses all of the fundamental areas in our brains and involves a cue, routine/response, and reward.

Remember I said that habits are cyclical in nature and that they require us to repeat behaviors and be rewarded for this behavior because it is the response that strengthens our routine behavior. What we haven't yet covered is the cue or the preceding action, environment, or stimulus that triggers us to begin our ritual or habitual behavior. Let's say I get up in the morning at 7 am, my alarm going off is the cue to get out of bed and begin my morning routine. I go through to my kitchen, switch on the coffee pot, and the soft beep of the machinery is my cue to pour my cup of coffee. Hopping into the shower, the warm water on my body is my cue to begin my gratitude protocol, recalling things that I enjoy or that make my life easier for 10 seconds. Likewise, when I begin my commute to work, placing my earphones into my ears is my cue to listen to my gratitude story... All within a mere hour of the day, we are presented with cues that trigger our automated behaviors. Take a moment to become consciously aware of just a small portion of a normal day, and it is apparent that things like brushing our teeth, putting on our shoes, or even getting to work don't require much conscious thought at all. But what happens when our car keys are not in their usual spot or the coffee machine is broken? Suddenly we need to engage our brains and think about what we will do to get back on track with our habits, right?

Without a cue for our behaviors, our habits can't be formed or reinforced. It's with these cues that we can begin to really solidify our gratitude protocols because we already know what small steps to take when forming the routine, and gratitude in itself produces the dopamine and serotonin we need to reward our behaviors. A great way to create cues for gratitude is to institute our protocols into existing habits and routines. If you're an early morning shower person, do a quick 10-second gratitude recall. If you commute to work, place your gratitude story on the top of your playlist, or if you're an afternoon walker, set a reminder to do a 5-minute gratitude and mindfulness walk. The opportunities to add gratitude into your everyday routines are practically endless, but you're going to need to think about it and choose a time when you're not distracted.

Let's run over habit-loop formation one more time: We need a cue to trigger our brains to begin a behavior, a routine which is the behavior or actions we do when acting habitually, and a reward that reinforces our behaviors and lets us know that our behaviors are creating a positive response within our brains.

The great thing about rewards is that they don't need to be physical. In fact, they shouldn't be, and we can encourage our new gratitude habits by ensuring we tap into the right types of rewards for our brains. This can be done by engaging in behaviors that normally bring a sense of enjoyment or satisfaction, by experiencing positive emotions, or by simply reveling in the awesomeness that is our personal growth and development. For example, you could reward your new healthy cooking habit with mindful eating or a 10-second gratitude session. Or, take a moment to mindfully look at your surroundings after practicing gratitude, pointing out all of the things in the area that make you feel happy, calm, proud, or content. These natural, intrinsic forms of reward will ensure our brains release the positive neurochemicals we need to solidify our behaviors while combating stress, inducing relaxation, and completely negating that, "I don't have time," excuse most of us use to get out of doing new or challenging things.

It's up to us to figure out what's going to work to get our brain actively engaged in creating a gratitude habit, but by consistently incorporating gratitude into our current routines, finetuning our intrinsic reward systems, and celebrating the progress we make, gratitude can become a part of our everyday lives in a short amount of time with minimal effort.

A. Dealing With the Tough Times and Our Negative Emotions

The gratitude protocol I've provided is, in itself, an incredibly powerful tool that will help to navigate tough times, especially when we're facing negative experiences. Proper gratitude helps us to shift our perspectives so that our brains don't ruminate on the bad things in our lives. When we ruminate, these negative emotions are placed on a loop, amplifying our experiences. Mindfulness and gratitude protocols help us to reframe our thoughts while still accepting that sometimes, life just throws curveballs and allows us to see our circumstances in a far more balanced way.

Of course, our ability to regulate our emotions also improves with proper gratitude practices, and the usually strong emotional responses we have to negative emotions become far less overwhelming. This is because our neural circuitry is wired toward positive emotions and the behaviors that help us to release dopamine and serotonin in our brains. This negative/positive emotional experience means our brains naturally seek out balance rather than swinging wildly from one extreme to another. In essence, our brains become more resilient, and the neural pathways that are associated with problem-solving and positive adaptive responses help us to persevere because our brains instinctively know that we will get through whatever is causing us distress.

All of this ensures our stress hormones, like cortisol and adrenaline, are kept in check, to which our body responds by maintaining a reasonable heart rate, calming our neurotransmitters, and modulating our other stress responses. We begin to see ourselves as the hero in our own lives instead of the villain, and we're far more likely to be empathetic toward our own struggles, turning inward for validation and acceptance rather than comparing ourselves to others. Proper gratitude protocols never minimize or invalidate our experience or the negative emotions we experience, but they do provide us with the framework we need to acknowledge and accept our life experiences without judgment.

And all of this is great, really it is, but what happens when we begin our gratitude protocols and life decides to stick a spanner in the works? I mean, if we've been practicing gratitude for a couple of days and things come undone, it's a little rough to expect ourselves to suddenly have built the resilience we need to deal with whatever it is we're dealing with in the beginning phases of our gratitude.

The first thing we need to acknowledge when it comes to our emotions is that they're neither negative nor positive—they're simply neurological processes that occur and then trigger physiological processes. Our ancient ancestors knew that our emotions occurred to warn us or urge us to take action, but as modern people, we can sometimes take our emotions for granted, labeling them and reliving them without ever truly paying proper attention to what our brains are trying to tell us. Added to this, we suppress our emotions because we have labeled them, negating not only their purpose and the physiological responses but also the long-term implications of properly assessing and dealing with our emotions. And look, I'm not saying this is your fault either! We're taught that being happy is good and being angry is bad or that we shouldn't be sad forever, and so we believe that negative emotions are bad and positive emotions are great. But ask anybody with a mood disorder what it feels like to be maniacally happy for an extended period of time, and they'll tell you it's the furthest thing from great. Sure, while they're in that state, it's okay, but it's exhausting because emotions are not designed to be sustained for a long time before we return to a baseline of either feeling good or bad.

The next thing we need to remember when dealing with our emotions is that they're regarded as "low-level" responses within our brains. This means they happen in the subcortical areas of our brain that are responsible for our evolutionary responses and the production of biochemicals that directly affect our physiology. Emotions are in our DNA, they're designed and developed to help us make quick assessments of our environment and to respond appropriately. The amygdala is primarily involved in the release of the neurotransmitters that recall a memory that lets us know if it is safe or not safe. Our emotions also have a much stronger effect on us when they have objective meaning. This means we will feel an emotion much stronger if we actually see danger rather than just feel it or perceive it. Neat, right?

In human beings, there are six basic emotions. These are anger, disgust, fear, happiness, sadness, and surprise. What's important to note here is these are just our initial emotions—they're the most basic responses we have to external and internal stimuli (Gu et al., 2019). When these emotions combine, eleven further emotions can be elicited, including

- amusement
- contempt
- contentment
- embarrassment
- excitement
- guilt
- pride
- relief
- satisfaction

- pleasure
- shame

Incidentally, we cannot remain in a state of our basic emotions. In other words, we cannot remain angry, but we can remain in a baseline state of these mixed emotions. So, if we get angry, this anger will subside and may give way to shame, guilt, or embarrassment. In recalling the memory of why we are in this baseline state, anger may flair again, but again, only temporarily. Everything else we feel on the spectrum of what we believe are emotions are actually feelings we develop toward our emotions, and these feelings, believe it or not, can last as long as we want them to. For us to be able to deal with our "negative" emotions, we need to understand that while we have no choice in experiencing them, they are there for a reason and that, quite often, that reason is based on the polar opposite of what we are feeling.

Back in the early 1900s, professor of medicine and psychology Robert Plutchik investigated and researched emotions and the lessons or messages they were trying to send to us. Throughout the course of this research, Plutchik discovered that each emotion had a polar opposite and that by tapping into these opposites, we could calm our responses to what we deemed negative emotions (Gu et al., 2019). In addition, Plutchik was able to label the varying degrees of the emotions we feel, making it much easier for us to assign a word to the emotions we experience.

Here's an example: Anger can be placed into varying degrees from rage, to anger, to annoyance. Fear can range from terror, to fear, to apprehension. Each of these varying degrees of emotions was placed on an easy-to-read color wheel with the polar opposite allowing us to properly ascertain what messages or actions needed to be addressed. It's a really amazing neurological and psychological reference point, and you should check it out to help gain more clarity. When we examine Plutchik's wheel, it becomes easier to see that perhaps our anger is borne from fear, or that our sadness requires us to seek out joy, or even that our disgust means we need to surround ourselves with people we can trust.

So how do we overcome our negative emotions? We don't! It's not normal for us to repress or move away from how we feel, even if these feelings are not particularly comfortable. When we ignore and suppress how we feel, it's at our own peril.

Our negative emotions are incredibly healthy and can be used as a helpful aid in ensuring we don't fall into this "joy trap" where we believe we need to be happy all the time to be grateful or to love our lives. We don't! As people, we need to experience a full range of emotions so that we can adapt to our circumstances while we grow and learn throughout the course of our lives. What we do need to do is learn to cope with our emotions better.

Okay, so now we know that emotions are low-level responses, and this means we can choose how we respond to them, and by using Plutchik's wheel, we can begin to understand how our negative emotions are sending us messages that can actually be of huge benefit to us. It's important that we seek out these messages, signals, and clues about what is not sitting right with us so that we can return to a baseline emotion that is acceptable to us. Mindfulness is an amazing way to examine our inner thoughts and feelings without judgment so that we can seek solutions rather than blaming others and ourselves for the perpetual emotional rollercoaster we're on.

Added to this, mindfulness is one of the most formidable allies we have in learning acceptance of our circumstances, but also our role in healing ourselves and improving our well-being. Accepting that we have negative emotions, and that they are part of being a person, will help us to develop self-compassion during the tough times we need to endure. Rather than becoming stuck in this mindset that everything bad always happens to us, we learn to accept that things are temporary and fleeting if we allow them to be.

Mindfulness also teaches us that emotions are not something to be feared and that our experiences are not wrong. This allows us to reframe how we feel and change how we react to the obstacles placed in our path. When combined with gratitude, acceptance becomes a powerful tool in helping us to develop meaningful behavior that helps us respond, not react, to our emotions so that they can begin to bring value to our lives as we seek out the lessons we need to learn from them.

B. Developing Gratitude: Self-Discipline When Motivation Wanes

You may remember that I said motivation is a necessary, but temporary, emotion that we all need to get started on projects or new tasks. Motivation is the key to getting started with new tasks and creating new habits, but it will inevitably wane, and specific strategies need to be put into place for goals to be achieved.

Without motivation, it's really difficult not only to institute new great habits but to overwrite the old bad habits we have created, and if you're one of those people who sprint out of the metaphorical gates only to lose steam on the first corner, you're going to want to listen up when it comes to this final section of the book.

We've all heard the age-old complaint, "I can't seem to stay motivated," and it's completely normal because motivation is not meant to be sustained. What we're looking to do is to sustain our motivation while we build self-discipline and tap into a little bit of renewed motivation when times get tough, or our old bad habits try to persistently push us to return to learned ways. To better understand how we can tap into motivation and sustain it while we are building self-discipline, it's important that we understand what motivation is and how we can align our goals with our values so that motivation is a natural process for us.

A simple definition of motivation is the intrinsic drive we tap into so that we can achieve something we need. This can be something physical or something intangible, like self-growth, a change in mindset, and so on. Our motivation is affected by a number of different variables, including how much we need the thing we're trying to achieve or obtain, what we will gain from our achievement, what we will lose, and what our personal expectations are.

The reason setting goals can be challenging is that, as people, we fear change, and as such, our motivation is affected by what we will lose and our personal expectations of changing overnight. Regardless of its temporary status, motivation is critical for anything new we begin in our lives because it provides us with a roadmap, helps us solve the obstacles and problems we face, and teaches us resilience as well as how to identify opportunities for success.

Getting motivated is one thing, and it's actually pretty simple—set an achievable goal, put a timeframe to this goal, and break this goal down into smaller, achievable steps that can be taken every day toward success. But what happens when motivation wanes because things begin to change, even if it's for the better, or other priorities become more important? The brakes are put on, and we set our goals aside for other things, usually the things that perpetuate or solidify our old bad habits.

So before we talk about how to sustain motivation and give a motivation boost, we need to examine how we can build self-discipline while our initial motivation levels are high. The first thing we need to do is to tap into the brain's need for patterns and routine. By instituting new habitual behaviors into existing patterns, we can modify our behaviors until, eventually, our new behaviors overtake our old ones.

Next, we need to silence that inner critic, challenging any conversation that begins with *what-if* or *should* and ends in a negative. All this is going to do is destroy motivation and have us stuck in a never-ending thought spiral. Try incorporating positive self-talk into daily practices so that depression and anxiety can be kept at bay and thought spirals are silenced more effectively.

Self-discipline relies heavily on resilience and our ability to problem-solve obstacles that come our way, and it's important that we build upon our resilience by challenging our brains rather than overwhelming them. We don't need to do everything all at once. In fact, small increments that move toward our goal of becoming grateful work far better than taking on everything and hoping for the best. Think of milestones as a way to build up tolerance and slowly become resilient to the challenges we face every day.

Right, so now that we know how to become self-disciplined, we can look at how to sustain our motivation for as long as possible and give ourselves a boost of motivation when we need it.

1. Set reminders for yourself until you no longer need a reminder. Having this reminder in place will ensure you are practicing gratitude when you should be. Remember, we're not looking for time, we're instituting gratitude into our existing time.
2. Review your milestones to see which of these are working for you and which may need replacing. If you really cannot listen to your gratitude story while commuting to work, there's no point in trying to force it. The nature of our gratitude protocol is that it can be fitted into any of your existing routines.
3. Stay away from definitive statements because they're great if you know for a fact they're true. If, however, there is even a slight chance of failure, using definitive statements can derail motivation and lead to ditching

gratitude altogether. Instead of saying, "I can't," or even "I can," change your language to, "I'll try."
4. Always prioritize rewarding yourself when you consistently achieve a milestone. The point of your gratitude journey is to ensure you're rewarding your brain as often as possible for your new, great behaviors.

For a motivation boost, take the time to remind yourself why you began your journey with neuroscience-backed gratitude practices. This will allow you to realign your purpose with your behavior. Take a look back on all of the milestones you've already achieved to give yourself a confidence and self-esteem boost. Remind yourself that new habits take as many as two months to form but that this is a short amount of time in the grander scheme of things, and make sure that you are persistently working toward rebuilding your brain. Remind yourself of your "*why*" in the moments you feel like giving up. This will help you build momentum when you feel like giving up. Finally, surround yourself with mentors and people who will help you reinforce your new habits and who are living a life of gratitude themselves. People who have a baseline that is more positive will be able to guide you and provide you with temporary motivation and, let's face it, there's nothing that drains your energy more than people who fixate on all of the bad things that happen in life.

Remember to focus on the benefits of your gratitude practice, review your goals often, and celebrate, celebrate, celebrate!

Yes, motivation is temporary, but self-discipline is permanent, and it's a valuable tool that will be used in every facet of your life. Motivation is needed to become self-disciplined and to change our lives for the better, and it's important that we acknowledge the intricate dance that happens between neuroscience, psychology, and action when we explore ways to grow in our lives.

Through Neuroscience's lens, we have discovered just how powerful gratitude is and the importance of a proper gratitude protocol. We have a deeper understanding of the neurological mechanisms required not only for gratitude but also for how we can tap into the power of mindfulness, motivation, and self-discipline in transforming our lives.

By making use of the knowledge you've gained throughout the course of this book, you now have the tools you need to build a strong, intentional gratitude practice that encourages physiological change as we reshape our habits and build resilience. By tapping into our brain's natural neuroplastic abilities, we open ourselves up to a world of opportunity for positive growth and development. While motivation is certainly an innate trait that is designed to help get us started with new habits and development, self-discipline is not, and we need to be able to nurture and motivate ourselves using the strategies provided for us to tap into the intricate web of our minds.

Motivation and self-discipline provide us with a robust scaffolding for our gratitude protocols, providing us with a sense of accomplishment and fulfillment as our brains begin to facilitate the behaviors needed for gratitude to become an automated process.

And there you have it! A clear vision, defined goals, the ability to motivate yourself and to remain disciplined, and a toolbox of techniques and instructions on how to harness the true power of proper gratitude. As you move on to the final chapter of this book and a recap of the information you've been provided with, I encourage you to embrace this new life and apply the knowledge you have learned.

Conclusion

Research conducted into the neuroscience of gratitude has provided us with profound insights into the impact of proper gratitude practice in our lives. In tapping into the natural, but intricate working of our brains, science shows that we have the power to transform our lives into one that is filled with joy and inner contentment.

The fascinating scientific evidence provided to us by cutting-edge technology and research interpretation demonstrates the true power of gratitude in our thought processes, and emotions, and in completely rewiring the neural circuitry of our brains. Current research is just the tip of the iceberg in my opinion, as neuroscientists conduct further studies into the potential modulation of the various regions of our brains.

True gratitude isn't about invalidating our experiences, or soul-searching for the great things in our lives when we know on some deeper level we are struggling. Instead, it's about understanding the enormous impact the gratitude we receive and give has on our ability to reduce our stress hormones and coax the release of dopamine and serotonin. Gratitude strengthens positive neural pathways, helping us to regulate our emotions and foster a mindset of acceptance, even in the most trying of times. As a result, we become more compassionate toward ourselves and others, foster resilience and tolerance, and create meaningful connections within ourselves and in our external relationships.

While we have covered the technical aspects of gratitude in great depth, it's important to know that even if nothing else is remembered from *The Neuroscience of Gratitude*, traditional gratitude simply doesn't work and that we all need the protocol explained in Chapter 4 to begin to feel the benefits of our long-forgotten gratitude emotion. Incorporating our protocol into everyday life will ensure we don't succumb to the fleeting whims of motivation, causing gratitude to become yet another thing that is a passing sentiment in our lives. We need to nurture and cultivate our gratitude protocols so that they create lasting physiological changes within our brains so that we can build sustained and prolonged habits in our lives.

And, if you're one of those people with a million things to do and even more thoughts in your mind, remember that Chapter 4 breaks down each of these gratitude protocol steps in easy-to-follow tables, and a specially designed journal is available to you so that you can easily practice your new gratitude protocol.

Neuroscience does confirm that habit formation works differently for different people and as such, the formation of our gratitude habits needs to be refined. We need to let go of the notion that creating a beneficial habit is a "one-size-fits-all" approach. Sure! The gratitude protocol provided works, but it's the habit formation where most people begin to battle. It's critical that we find what resonates most deeply with us when it comes to instituting gratitude into our lives, choosing gratitude habits that fit within our purpose and our values as well as our schedule.

You've now been given the tools to tap into your brain, maximizing your potential to reignite gratitude and changing your neural circuitry, and improving the way your brain works. Now is the time to embrace this knowledge, putting it to use in your life so that you can create a transformative protocol that embraces mindfulness and intention. Gratitude is not about seeking out the things that are going well in your life—it's the ability to acknowledge that perceptions are valid and that life is hard sometimes but there are people who *appreciate* you and express their *gratitude* toward you.

So, as you move forward on this journey, may this journey of gratitude proven by neuroscience inspire you to create your own path to a grateful life. May it become the catalyst to lasting personal growth and lasting well-being, and may you unlock a life that is fulfilling and joyful for you.

One Final Note

Dear Reader,

I'm Andrew Humington, the author of this book.

Thank you again for your trust in sharing this journey with me, and I truly hope my work will have a positive impact on your life and help you succeed.

Writing this book was both challenging and enjoyable, and I genuinely hope you've gained valuable insights from our time together.

Before we part ways, I'd like to share something important:As a self-published author, I don't have the backing of a large publishing house with extensive advertising budgets or widespread promotional campaigns.

This book stems from my passion for neuroscience and my desire to share its findings to benefit as many people as possible.

I sincerely hope it helps you fulfill your potential.

Now, it's my turn to request a small favor from you:

Reviews are vital for us, as they help prevent our book from being lost in the vast sea of Amazon rankings and ensure it remains visible to potential readers.

Your completion of this book is already more than I could ask for, but if you could spare just a minute to leave a review on Amazon, it would mean the world to me.

Regardless, thank you once again for placing your trust in me and giving this book a chance.

If you're interested in learning more about recent neuroscience discoveries and how they can help you transform your life, I plan to publish additional works on various topics within the **Neuromastery Lab collection** (available on Amazon and Audible).

I hope to see you there!

Wishing you a fantastic day, and a heartfelt thank you if you decide to leave a review.

Andrew Humington

Glossary

Amygdala: The amygdalae (plural) are two very small but complex almond-shaped neural clusters located near the base of the brain that play an important role in communications with other brain regions. The amygdala is primarily involved in memory, emotion, and the sympathetic nervous system response to risks and dangers.

Cerebral cortex: The outermost portion of the brain, separated into four major lobes: The frontal lobe, associated with cognition; the parietal lobe, which processes sensory information; the occipital lobe, responsible for visual processing, and the temporal lobe, responsible for creation and preservation of memory, auditory perception, and language recognition.

Dopamine: A monoamine neurotransmitter or chemical messenger between neurons in the brain and parts of the body. It functions as a neurohormone that the hypothalamus releases within the brain and plays a role as a "reward center" in memory, movement, motivation, mood, and attention.

Fight-or-flight: A response to danger that evolved to help our prehistoric ancestors react quickly when imminent threats required extra speed and strength. It is triggered by the sympathetic nervous system, which increases heart and breathing rates, raises blood pressure, and stops digestion to conserve energy.

Limbic system: Parts of the brain responsible for all emotional experiences, consisting of the prefrontal cortex, thalamus, hypothalamus, amygdala, hippocampus, ventral tegmental area, and cingulate gyrus.

Mysticism: From the Greek word for "initiate" or "to set in motion." "Mysticism is popularly known as becoming one with God or the Absolute but may refer to any kind of ecstasy or altered state of consciousness which is given a religious or spiritual meaning" (Wikipedia, 2023). Mysticism can also be the attainment of deep insights.

Myths: There are many misconceptions and misunderstandings advocated by self-help advocates. Common myths about practicing gratitude include misunderstanding the effectiveness of generic techniques, and believing that all gratitude practices are equal in effectiveness in creating a beneficial effect.

Narrative: An effective gratitude practice is grounded in a narrative, or a story of you (or another you observe) receiving deep feelings of gratitude from another or others. It needs to be sincere to evoke positive physical and psychological responses. Successful gratitude can be achieved with a compelling narrative.

Neuroscience: The science-based review of the medical evidence of the effectiveness of gratitude, and the physiological changes it creates in the brain. Three regions of the brain are involved: The prefrontal cortex; the amygdala; and the ventral tegmental area. Neurochemicals associated with gratitude are dopamine, oxytocin, and serotonin.

Optimism: The attitude that perceives all aspects of life favorably, and that everything will work out for the best. An optimist interprets setbacks as having value in teaching lessons so that next time you'll do it right or at least better. Sooner or later, the situation will be resolved.

Oxytocin: A neuropeptide hormone produced in the hypothalamus and released by the pituitary gland. Oxytocin evolved to improve the formation of relationships, and is recognized as a social bonding and caring enhancer, often called the "love hormone." It is produced in our bodies when we feel love and deep affection.

Positivity: Always believing in, and expecting success, while never believing in failure or defeat because most obstacles are mental in character. Positive thinking is thought to change one's outlook on life and lead to contentment and inner peace.

Prefrontal cortex: A large part of the brain, situated at the anterior of the frontal lobe, directly behind the forehead. This region influences and processes behavior, the ability to plan and make decisions, and helps form the personality.

Resilience: The ability to overcome setbacks, failures, errors, mistakes, and disappointments, and move on without regret. This is not denial, but is an aspect of positivism; believing in yourself, and not allowing frustration or guilt to dominate your thinking.

Self-values: Self-esteem is your perception of who you really are. It is close to self-confidence but more based on reality than imagination. Self-worth is more of an assessment of how you stand relative to others. Self-confidence is the degree of inner resolve and belief in one's ability to achieve objectives.

Serotonin: Like dopamine, serotonin is a neurotransmitter whose primary role is communicating between neurons in your brain and various parts of the body. Serotonin is produced in the brain from the amino acid tryptophan hydroxylase and its principal function is to stabilize mood, and feelings of happiness and well-being. It also plays a role in digestion and sleep cycles.

Transformation: Gratitude has transformative power which can contribute to personal growth by raising self-awareness and emotional intelligence, building your resilience and ability to cope with challenges, and encouraging overall personal development and self-improvement.

Ventral Tegmental Area: Located in the midbrain, it is the uppermost part of the brainstem that connects the upper brain to the spinal column, and is positioned adjacent to the substantia nigra.

References

Ackerman, C. (2018, July 25). *What is Neuroplasticity? A Psychologist Explains [+14 Exercises]*. Positive Psychology. https://positivepsychology.com/neuroplasticity/

Algoe, S., Gable, S., Maisel, N., David, M., Garcia, R., Huang, G., Legate, N., Madanipour, M., & Nguyen, J. (2010). It's the little things. *Biobehavioral Issues in Physical and Mental Health, 17*, 217–233. https://greatergood.berkeley.edu/images/uploads/Algoe-Gable-Maisel-2010-Its-the-little-things.pdf

Andrew Huberman. (2021, November 25). *Episode 47: The Science Of Gratitude & How To Build Gratitude Practice*. Podcast Notes. https://podcastnotes.org/huberman-lab/episode-47-the-science-of-gratitude-how-to-build-gratitude-practice-huberman-lab/

Bartlett, M. Y., & DeSteno, D. (2006). Gratitude and Prosocial Behavior. *Psychological Science, 17*(4), 319–325. https://doi.org/10.1111/j.1467-9280.2006.01705.x

Chaplin, L. N., John, D. R., Rindfleisch, A., & Froh, J. J. (2018). The impact of gratitude on adolescent materialism and generosity. *The Journal of Positive Psychology, 1–10*. https://doi.org/10.1080/17439760.2018.1497688

Crum, J. (2021). Understanding Mental Health and Cognitive Restructuring With Ecological

Neuroscience. *Frontiers in Psychiatry, 12.* https://doi.org/10.3389/fpsyt.2021.697095

Damasio, A., & Carvalho, G. B. (2013). The nature of feelings: evolutionary and neurobiological origins. *Nature Reviews Neuroscience, 14*(2), 143–152. https://doi.org/10.1038/nrn3403

Fox, G. (2017, August 4). *What Can the Brain Reveal about Gratitude?* Greater Good. https://greatergood.berkeley.edu/article/item/what_can_the_brain_reveal_about_gratitude

Fritz, M. M., Armenta, C. N., Walsh, L. C., & Lyubomirsky, S. (2019). Gratitude facilitates healthy eating behavior in adolescents and young adults. *Journal of Experimental Social Psychology, 81,* 4–14. https://doi.org/10.1016/j.jesp.2018.08.011

Gillette, H. (2023, March 6). *Can I Form a New Habit In 21 Days?* Psych Central. https://psychcentral.com/health/need-to-form-a-new-habit#:~:text=Habit%20formation%20can%20take%20an

Gu, S., Wang, F., Patel, N. P., Bourgeois, J. A., & Huang, J. H. (2019). A Model for Basic Emotions Using Observations of Behavior in Drosophila. *Frontiers in Psychology, 10*(781). https://doi.org/10.3389/fpsyg.2019.00781

Harvard Health Publishing. (2021, August 14). *Giving thanks can make you happier.* Harvard Health.

https://www.health.harvard.edu/healthbeat/giving-thanks-can-make-you-happier

Hasson, U., Feliú-Mójer, M. I., Yehuda, R., Zarate, J. M., & Suzuki, W. A. (2018). Dialogues: *The Science and Power of Storytelling. The Journal of Neuroscience, 38*(44), 9468–9470. https://doi.org/10.1523/jneurosci.1942-18.2018

Hori, D., Sasahara, S., Doki, S., Oi, Y., & Matsuzaki, I. (2020). *Prefrontal activation while listening to a letter of gratitude read aloud by a coworker face-to-face: A NIRS study.* PLOS ONE. https://doi.org/10.1371/journal.pone.0238715

Josep Calbet. (2018, March 14). *The Hebb´s rule explained with an analogy.* Neuroquotient. https://neuroquotient.com/en/pshychology-and-neuroscience-hebb-principle-rule/

Karns, C. M., Moore, W. E., & Mayr, U. (2017). The Cultivation of Pure Altruism via Gratitude: A Functional MRI Study of Change with Gratitude Practice. *Frontiers in Human Neuroscience, 11.* https://doi.org/10.3389/fnhum.2017.00599

Kini, P., Wong, J., McInnis, S., Gabana, N., & Brown, J. W. (2016). The effects of gratitude expression on neural activity. *NeuroImage, 128*, 1–10. https://doi.org/10.1016/j.neuroimage.2015.12.040

Kong, F., Zhao, J., You, X., & Xiang, Y. (2019). *Gratitude and the brain: Trait gratitude mediates the association between structural variations in the medial prefrontal cortex and life satisfaction*. Emotion. https://doi.org/10.1037/emo0000617

Krause, E. D., Mendelson, T., & Lynch, T. R. (2003). Childhood emotional invalidation and adult psychological distress: the mediating role of emotional inhibition. *Child Abuse & Neglect, 27*(2), 199–213. https://doi.org/10.1016/s0145-2134(02)00536-7

Kyeong, S., Kim, J., Kim, D. J., Kim, H. E., & Kim, J.-J. (2017). Effects of gratitude meditation on neural network functional connectivity and brain-heart coupling. *Scientific Reports, 7*(1). https://doi.org/10.1038/s41598-017-05520-9

Lang, P. J. (2010). Emotion and Motivation: Toward Consensus Definitions and a Common Research Purpose. *Emotion Review, 2*(3), 229–233. https://doi.org/10.1177/1754073910361984

Liu, Y.-Z., Wang, Y.-X., & Jiang, C.-L. (2017). Inflammation: The Common Pathway of Stress-Related Diseases. *Frontiers in Human Neuroscience, 11*(316). https://doi.org/10.3389/fnhum.2017.00316

Marquit, M. (2023, March 22). *How gratitude can help your finances*. IG Wealth Management. https://www.ig.ca/en/insights/how-gratitude-can-help-your-finances

Nazarian, V. (2004). *Vera Nazarian Quote*. A-Z Quotes. https://www.azquotes.com/quote/372781

Powers, A., Stevens, J. S., van Rooij, S. J. H., Ely, T. D., Fani, N., Jovanovic, T., Ressler, K. J., & Bradley, B. (2017). Neural correlates and structural markers of emotion dysregulation in traumatized civilians. *Social Cognitive and Affective Neuroscience, 12*(5), 823–831. https://doi.org/10.1093/scan/nsx005

Sansone, R. A., & Sansone, L. A. (2019). Gratitude and well being: the benefits of appreciation. *Psychiatry (Edgmont), 7*(11), 18–22. https://www.ncbi.nlm.nih.gov/pmc/articles/PMC3010965/

Schipani, D. (2018, October 16). *Here's How Stress and Inflammation Are Linked.* Everyday Health. https://www.everydayhealth.com/wellness/united-states-of-stress/link-between-stress-inflammation/

Schuman-Olivier, Z., Trombka, M., Lovas, D. A., Brewer, J. A., Vago, D. R., Gawande, R., Dunne, J. P., Lazar, S. W., Loucks, E. B., & Fulwiler, C. (2020). Mindfulness and Behavior Change. *Harvard Review of Psychiatry, 28*(6), 371–394. https://doi.org/10.1097/HRP.0000000000000277

Tang, Y.-Y., & Leve, L. D. (2016). A translational neuroscience perspective on mindfulness meditation as a prevention strategy. *Translational Behavioral Medicine, 6*(1), 63–72. https://doi.org/10.1007/s13142-015-0360-x

University of Utah. (2021, November 19). *Practicing Gratitude for Better Health and Well-Being.* University of Utah Health.

https://healthcare.utah.edu/healthfeed/2021/11/practicing-gratitude-better-health-and-well-being

Wood, A. M., Froh, J. J., & Geraghty, A. W. A. (2010). Gratitude and well-being: A review and theoretical integration. *Clinical Psychology Review, 30*(7), 890–905. https://doi.org/10.1016/j.cpr.2010.03.005

Zahn, R., Garrido, G., Moll, J., & Grafman, J. (2013). Individual differences in posterior cortical volume correlate with proneness to pride and gratitude. *Social Cognitive and Affective Neuroscience, 9*(11), 1676–1683. https://doi.org/10.1093/scan/nst158

Zielinski, M. J., & Veilleux, J. C. (2018). The Perceived Invalidation of Emotion Scale (PIES): Development and psychometric properties of a novel measure of current emotion invalidation. *Psychological Assessment, 30*(11), 1454–1467. https://doi.org/10.1037/pas0000584

Made in the USA
Columbia, SC
15 December 2023